Verse by Verse Commentary on the Book of

DANIEL

Enduring Word Commentary Series
By David Guzik

The grass withers, the flower fades,
but the word of our God stands forever.
Isaiah 40:8

Commentary on Daniel

Copyright ©2019 by David Guzik

Printed in the United States of America or in the United Kingdom

Print Edition ISBN: 1-56599-036-6

Enduring Word

5662 Calle Real #184

Goleta, CA 93117

Originally published in 2005, updated in 2019

Electronic Mail: ewm@enduringword.com

Internet Home Page: www.enduringword.com

Scripture references, unless noted, are from the New King James Version of the Bible, copyright ©1979, 1980, 1982, Thomas Nelson, Inc., Publisher.

Contents

*Dedicated
with gratitude
to Ricky Ryan*

Daniel 1 - Keeping Pure in The Face of Adversity

A. Introduction to the Book of Daniel.

1. Setting the time: The prophet Daniel lived in the sixth century before the birth of Jesus. During this approximate period:

- Construction began on the Acropolis in Athens.
- Mayan civilization flourished in Mexico.
- Aesop wrote his fables.
- Confucius and Buddha lived.
- Greek art began to truly excel.
- The Greeks introduced the olive tree to Italy.
- The Phoenicians made the first known sea journey around Africa.

2. The Book of Daniel is a target of critics who doubt that the Daniel described in the book actually wrote the book, especially in light of the book's amazing prophecies.

a. The Book of Daniel *claims* to be written by Daniel himself, and the fact that it is written mostly in the third person does not contradict that claim.

i. The author mostly speaks in the third person, except for Daniel 8:1, 9:2, 9:20, and 10:2, where he speaks in the "I, Daniel" form. However, it was customary for ancient writers to speak in the third person even when writing about themselves. The one Old Testament exception to this is the Book of Nehemiah, which is in the form of a personal diary.

ii. Even God switches between the grammatical first and third person when speaking of Himself. One can compare Exodus 20:2 (*I am the LORD your God*) and Exodus 20:7 (*for the LORD will not hold him guiltless*).

iii. Fortunately, Jesus took away all doubt on the matter. *He* told us that Daniel wrote the book of Daniel: *Therefore when you see the 'abomination of desolation,' spoken of by Daniel the prophet* (Matthew 24:15 and Mark 13:14).

b. The Book of Daniel predicts events of the second century before the coming of Jesus (especially the period 175-164 B.C.) with such precision that doubting critics believe it *had* to have been written *after* that period, during the time of the Maccabees (in-between the Old and New Testaments). Supposedly, the purpose for writing Daniel at that time was to inspire God's people on to victory during the Maccabean wars.

i. The first recorded suggestion for a Maccabean date for Daniel was by the Neoplatonic philosopher Porphyrius of Tyre (third century A.D.). Porphyrius couldn't believe the prophecies, so he suggested the later date. An early Christian writer and scholar named Jerome refuted these arguments in his commentary on Daniel.

ii. Influenced by Enlightenment philosophies, academics began to revive the old Maccabean date theory about the Book of Daniel. There was consensus among many academics that every accurate prediction in Daniel was written after the events took place.

c. The modern argument for late dating Daniel is based on supposed inevitable mistakes that a second century B.C. writer made when writing about a period 400 years before, in the sixth century B.C. In our own day, it would be as if someone wrote a story about the Pilgrims landing at Plymouth Rock while mentioning speedboats and computers. We would know that it was a forgery. There are usually said to be five main historical blunders:

- The date for Nebuchadnezzar's invasion of Judah.
- Using the word *Chaldeans* to describe a class of soothsayers.
- The account of Nebuchadnezzar's madness.
- King Belshazzar and his relationship to Nabonidus.
- The figure of Darius the Mede.

i. There is also a linguistic argument made against the Book of Daniel, claiming that certain Greek words used in Daniel are words that did not come into the Hebrew vocabulary until the second century B.C.

3. (1-2) Nebuchadnezzar conquers Jerusalem.

In the third year of the reign of Jehoiakim king of Judah, Nebuchadnezzar king of Babylon came to Jerusalem and besieged it. And the Lord gave Jehoiakim king of Judah into his hand, with some of the articles of the

house of God, which he carried into the land of Shinar to the house of his god; and he brought the articles into the treasure house of his god.

a. **Jehoiakim king of Judah**: This was a Judean king placed on the throne by the Pharaoh of Egypt. His name means "Yahweh raises up," but the LORD did not raise him up at all - Pharaoh did.

b. **Nebuchadnezzar king of Babylon**: This was the mighty ruler of the Babylonian Empire. The name **Nebuchadnezzar** is a Hebrew transliteration of the Babylonian name *Nebu-kudduri-utzur*, which means "Nebu protects the crown."

c. **Came to Jerusalem and besieged it**: Nebuchadnezzar came against Jerusalem because the Pharaoh of Egypt invaded Babylon. In response, the young prince Nebuchadnezzar defeated the Egyptians at Charchemish, then he pursued their fleeing army all the way down to the Sinai. Along the way (or on the way back), he subdued Jerusalem, which had been loyal to the Pharaoh of Egypt.

i. This happened in 605 B.C. and it was the first (but not the last) encounter between Nebuchadnezzar and Jehoiakim. There would be two later invasions (597 and 587 B.C.).

ii. Some say that this mention of the siege of Jerusalem is a historical blunder made by a pseudo-Daniel. This is based on the fact that this invasion in 605 B.C. is not mentioned in the book of Kings. But the Jewish historian Josephus quotes the Babylonian historian Berossus, showing that the Biblical account of three separate Babylonian attacks on Judah is accurate (*Against Apion,* I 19 and *Antiquities*, X 11, 1).

iii. This specific attack mentioned by Daniel is documented by the Babylonian Chronicles, a collection of tablets discovered as early as 1887 and kept in the British Museum. Nebuchadnezzar's 605 B.C. presence in Judah is documented and clarified in these tablets.

iv. When the Babylonian Chronicles were finally published in 1956, they gave us first-rate, detailed political and military information about the first 10 years of Nebuchadnezzar's reign. L.W. King prepared these tablets in 1919. He then died, and they were neglected for four decades.

v. Excavations also document the victory of Nebuchadnezzar over the Egyptians at Carchemish in May or June of 605 B.C. Archaeologists found evidence of battle, vast quantities of arrowheads, layers of ash, and the shield of a Greek mercenary fighting for the Egyptians.

vi. This campaign of Nebuchadnezzar was interrupted suddenly when he heard of his father's death and raced back to Babylon to secure his succession to the throne. He traveled about 500 miles in two weeks - remarkable speed for travel in that day.

vii. Therefore, we know that the siege of Jerusalem in 605 B.C. was cut short by Nebuchadnezzar's return to Babylon. This was not specifically detailed in the Babylonian Chronicles, but it is entirely consistent with the record.

d. **In the third year of the reign**: There is also no contradiction between Daniel (who said this happened in the **third year of** Jehoiakim) and Jeremiah 46:2 (which said it was *in the fourth year of Jehoiakim*). Daniel reckoned a king's years after the Babylonian method: the first year of a king's reign began at the start of the calendar year *after* he took the throne. Jeremiah used the Jewish method.

i. "It was customary for the Babylonians to consider the first year of a king's reign as the year of accession and to call the next year the first year... Having spent most of his life in Babylon, it is only natural that Daniel should use a Babylonian form of chronology." (Walvoord)

e. **And the Lord gave Jehoiakim king of Judah into his hand**: In this 597 B.C. deportation **Jehoiakim**, Ezekiel, and others were taken away. This deportation is described in 2 Kings 24:14-16.

i. This was prophesied in Isaiah 39:7: *And they shall take away some of your sons who will descend from you, whom you will beget; and they shall be eunuchs in the palace of the king of Babylon.* This prophecy leads some to think Daniel and his companions were made eunuchs. Certainly, the Hebrew term *saris* was used of literal eunuchs; but the word derives from a phrase that simply means to be a servant of the king. It wasn't exclusively applied to literal eunuchs.

ii. The LORD gave Judah into the hands of the Babylonians for mainly two reasons. The first was Israel's idolatry and the second was their failure to observe the Sabbaths for the land (Leviticus 25:1-7 and 26:2-35). This shows that God always settles accounts with those who refuse to respond to His warnings. In the 587 B.C. invasion the city of Jerusalem and the temple were destroyed (2 Kings 25:9-10).

f. **Some of the articles of the house of God**: Nebuchadnezzar did not take *all* the furnishings of the temple, only **some**. The remaining furnishings were either hidden before Nebuchadnezzar came or they were brought to Babylon later.

i. The confiscation of these items and their deposit in a Babylonian temple was a dramatic declaration by Nebuchadnezzar saying, "my god is better than your God." Now the God of Israel had to vindicate Himself.

ii. This was a low time for Judah and God's people. It seemed that the God of Israel lost out to the gods of Assyria, Egypt, and Babylon. The Book of Daniel shows God vindicating Himself at a time when the conquest of Israel might have brought God's reputation into disgrace.

B. Babylon's system of indoctrination.

1. (3-4) The best and the brightest of Jerusalem's young men are chosen and taken to Babylon.

Then the king instructed Ashpenaz, the master of his eunuchs, to bring some of the children of Israel and some of the king's descendants and some of the nobles, young men in whom *there was* no blemish, but good-looking, gifted in all wisdom, possessing knowledge and quick to understand, who *had* ability to serve in the king's palace, and whom they might teach the language and literature of the Chaldeans.

a. **Bring some of the children of Israel**: Nebuchadnezzar not only confiscated holy things from the temple but also the shining lights of Judah's future (young men perhaps 13 to 17 years old).

i. Walvoord on the phrase **king's descendants**: "The Hebrew for *the princes* is a Persian word, *partemim*, which is cited as another proof for a late date of Daniel. However, inasmuch as Daniel lived in his latter years under Persian government as a high official, there is nothing strange about an occasional Persian word."

b. **Who had the ability to serve in the king's palace**: Nebuchadnezzar demonstrated that he was a wise administrator and a shrewd tactician. Taking these young men as hostages reminded the people back in Jerusalem that they should not revolt against the recently imposed Babylonian rule.

2. (5-7) In Babylon, the Hebrew youths are groomed for the civil service.

And the king appointed for them a daily provision of the king's delicacies and of the wine which he drank, and three years of training for them, so that at the end of *that time* they might serve before the king. Now from among those of the sons of Judah were Daniel, Hananiah, Mishael, and Azariah. To them the chief of the eunuchs gave names: he gave Daniel *the name* Belteshazzar; to Hananiah, Shadrach; to Mishael, Meshach; and to Azariah, Abed-Nego.

a. **The king appointed for them a daily provision of the king's delicacies**: It was a given that the Babylonian government would provide for these young men in training. Yet, having the same food and wine prepared for the king was intended to be a special honor.

i. In the ancient world much more than in the modern world there was a huge difference between the food enjoyed by the elite and what common people ate.

b. **To them the chief of the eunuchs gave names**: Daniel tells us about four of these youths, and their new Babylonian names.

i. The name **Daniel** (meaning *God is my judge*) was changed to **Belteshazzar** (meaning *Bel's prince*).

ii. The name **Hannaniah** (meaning *Beloved by the LORD*) was changed to **Shadrach** (meaning *Illumined by Sun-god*).

iii. The name **Mishael** (meaning *Who is as God*) was changed to **Meshach** (meaning *Who is like Venus*).

iv. The name **Azariah** (meaning *The LORD is my help*) was changed to **Abed-Nego** (meaning *Servant of Nego*).

c. **Three years of training for them**: The purpose of the food, names, and education was simple. This was an effort at total indoctrination, with the goal of making these young Jewish men leave behind their Hebrew God and culture. Undoubtedly, Nebuchadnezzar wanted to communicate to these young men, "look to *me* for everything." Daniel and his friends refused, insisting that they would look to God.

i. Calvin wrote that Nebuchadnezzar knew that the Jews were a stiff-necked and obstinate people, and that he used the sumptuous food to soften up the captives.

ii. Satan uses a similar strategy against believers today, wanting to indoctrinate us into the world system. Satan wants us to:

- Identify (name) us in reference to the world.
- Feed us what the world offers.
- Educate us in the ways of the world.

3. (8) Daniel's decision to be faithful.

But Daniel purposed in his heart that he would not defile himself with the portion of the king's delicacies, nor with the wine which he drank; therefore he requested of the chief of the eunuchs that he might not defile himself.

a. **That he would not defile himself**: The ancient Hebrew word **defile** carries the thought of *polluting* or *staining* (see also Isaiah 59:3, Zephaniah 3:1, and Malachi 1:7). That Daniel **requested** that he might not **defile**

himself implies that he explained the *spiritual* basis for his request. He didn't make it seem that he wanted to avoid the king's food out of other reasons.

i. **Therefore he requested**: Daniel made a big deal over a little thing. The only way to go on with God is to be faithful in little things. We might ask, "Daniel, why bring religion into it?" But Daniel realized that his relationship with God touched every area of his life, including what he ate. Significantly, the root of sin goes back to eating forbidden food.

b. **That he might not defile himself**: Daniel and his friends considered the king's food defiled for at least three reasons. First, it undoubtedly was not kosher. Second, it was probably sacrificed to idols. Third, eating the king's food implied fellowship with Babylon's cultural system.

i. Daniel did not object to the name given to him, because he knew who he was and others could call him what they wanted. Daniel did not object to the Babylonian education, because he knew what he believed. Daniel *did* object to the food from the king's table because eating it was direct disobedience to God's word.

ii. "By eastern standards to share a meal was to commit one's self to friendship; it was of covenant significance." (Baldwin)

iii. **Nor with the wine which he drank**: God did not forbid drinking **wine**. Nevertheless, in pagan cultures most wine and meat was dedicated to the gods, so Daniel and his friends refused it.

c. **Therefore he requested**: Daniel made a remarkably courageous decision, especially when we think of all the reasons why it was a hard decision to make.

i. The *king* ordered the menu. Rejecting the menu was rejecting the king, and could result in severe punishment.

ii. Refusing the food might have branded them as being *uncooperative*, and could have *spoiled all chances of advancement* (many other Hebrew youths *did* eat the food).

iii. There was a *real threat of punishment*. Ancient kings were well known for the severe and often sadistic punishments against those who crossed them. Nebuchadnezzar was capable of great cruelty. He murdered the sons of one king of Judah before the king's eyes then immediately gouged out the eyes of the king, so his last memory would always be the murder of his sons (Jeremiah 39:6-7). Other rulers of Judah were literally roasted to death over a fire (Jeremiah 29:22).

iv. The *food itself* was no doubt pretty attractive, and seemed a much better alternative than eating a vegetarian diet and water for three years.

v. Mere *distance* made this challenging. Separated from family and home, it was easy to compromise.

vi. It was easy to *think that God had let them down* by allowing them to be carried away into Babylon. These exiles, kidnapped from Jerusalem, might have said: "Why should we risk our neck for a God who let me down?" Yet they were committed to obedience even if God did not fulfill their expectations.

d. **Daniel purposed in his heart**: In this, Daniel illustrated how to conquer a difficult trial and glorify God before others in the midst of testing.

i. First, *the heart must be set*. Daniel **purposed in his heart**, making up his mind *beforehand* that he would not compromise.

ii. The *life must be positive*. Daniel found favor with his superiors.

iii. *Protest must be courteous*. Daniel **requested** to be excused from the king's table. He made a polite request, showing discretion. Making a stand for Jesus Christ does not mean we must be obnoxious.

iv. *Self-denial must be sought*. Daniel and his friends knew this would *cost* them something, yet they were willing. "Be ready for a bad name; be willing to be called a bigot; be prepared for the loss of friendships; be prepared for anything so long as you can stand fast by Him who bought you with His precious blood." (Spurgeon)

v. The *test must be boldly put*. "I think that a Christian man should be willing to be tried; he should be pleased to let his religion be put to the test. 'There,' says he, 'hammer away if you like.' Do you want to be carried to heaven on a feather bed? Do you want always to be protected from everybody's sneer and frown; and to go to heaven as if you were riding in the procession on Lord Mayor's day?" (Spurgeon)

C. The results of Daniel's courageous decision.

1. (9) God gave Daniel **favor and goodwill** with the authorities.

Now God had brought Daniel into the favor and goodwill of the chief of the eunuchs.

a. **God had brought Daniel into the favor**: God did not abandon those who stood for Him. Daniel entrusted himself to God and God came through - though it was no doubt a stretching experience for Daniel and his friends.

b. **Into the favor and goodwill of the chief**: God moved upon the authorities so they regarded Daniel with **goodwill**; but God also worked through the wise actions of Daniel to cultivate this goodwill.

2. (10-13) Daniel suggests a plan.

And the chief of the eunuchs said to Daniel, "I fear my lord the king, who has appointed your food and drink. For why should he see your faces looking worse than the young men who *are* your age? Then you would endanger my head before the king." So Daniel said to the steward whom the chief of the eunuchs had set over Daniel, Hananiah, Mishael, and Azariah, "Please test your servants for ten days, and let them give us vegetables to eat and water to drink. "Then let our appearance be examined before you, and the appearance of the young men who eat the portion of the king's delicacies; and as you see fit, *so* deal with your servants."

a. **Please test your servants**: Daniel saw the situation through the steward's eyes and addressed *his* legitimate concerns. He wouldn't let the chief of the eunuchs pay the price for Daniel's conscience. In it all, Daniel was willing to put himself and his faith in God to the test.

i. There was something so *reasonable* about Daniel's approach. He could have gone on a hunger strike or made some other kind of protest. Instead he made a polite request, he made it to the right person and said, "Put us to the test."

ii. In this sense we might say that Daniel made a godly and wise *compromise* with the **chief of the eunuchs**. He certainly did not compromise in an ungodly way, but he showed the wisdom James 3:17 speaks of: *But the wisdom that is from above is first pure, then peaceable, gentle, **willing to yield**, full of mercy and good fruits, without partiality and without hypocrisy.*

iii. "Martyrs by proxy, who have such strong convictions that they think it somebody else's duty to run risk for them, are by no means unknown." (Maclaren)

iv. "It is of no use for a man to say, 'I have made up my mind upon certain things,' and to keep doggedly fighting over those matters, while, at the same time, the whole of his life is unkind, ungenerous, and unlovable. Yes, by all manner of means be a martyr if you like; but do not martyr everybody else." (Spurgeon)

b. **Vegetables to eat and water to drink**: **Vegetables** refers to all kinds of grains and plants, not strictly vegetables. Basically, this was a vegetarian diet, chosen because the meat at the king's table was not prepared in a kosher manner or it was sacrificed to idols.

> i. Daniel was not presumptuous and he did not wrongly test God in this situation, because he had both a command to obey and a promise to trust. Exodus 23:25 says, *So you shall serve the* Lord *your God, and He will bless your bread and your water.*

3. (14-16) Daniel and his companions are blessed for their faithfulness.

So he consented with them in this matter, and tested them ten days. And at the end of ten days their features appeared better and fatter in flesh than all the young men who ate the portion of the king's delicacies. Thus the steward took away their portion of delicacies and the wine that they were to drink, and gave them vegetables.

> a. **So he consented with them in this matter**: This was the hand of God at work. The chief of the eunuchs had all the power in this situation. Daniel and his friends seemed to be completely at his mercy. Yet God moved upon this man, and **he consented with them in this matter**.

> b. **Their features appeared better and fatter**: This was the hand of God at work. There was no *biological* reason why a vegetarian diet should make them appear **better and fatter**. Perhaps their diet would make them appear the *same* as the other Jewish young men who ate the king's food, but not **better and fatter**.

4. (17-21) Daniel and his companions are blessed and promoted.

As for these four young men, God gave them knowledge and skill in all literature and wisdom; and Daniel had understanding in all visions and dreams. Now at the end of the days, when the king had said that they should be brought in, the chief of the eunuchs brought them in before Nebuchadnezzar. Then the king interviewed them, and among them all none was found like Daniel, Hananiah, Mishael, and Azariah; therefore they served before the king. And in all matters of wisdom *and* understanding about which the king examined them, he found them ten times better than all the magicians *and* astrologers who *were* in all his realm. Thus Daniel continued until the first year of King Cyrus.

> a. **God gave them knowledge and skill**: The special intellectual ability of Daniel and his companions was not due to their diet, but to the special intervention of the Lord.

> > i. Some think their diet had a direct effect on their knowledge. Trapp says, "This slender diet was some help to their studies; for loaden bellies make leaden wits." Nevertheless, the key was certainly *spiritual*.

ii. These young Jewish men *gave themselves to the* L<small>ORD</small> in a remarkable way and God *blessed them* in a remarkable way. J. Edwin Orr remembered something Billy Brice said to him: "Edwin, if Christians would only give over and above their reasonable service, the Lord would give over and above the usual blessing." Daniel and his friends understood this principle, and God blessed them for acting on it.

b. **Daniel had understanding in all visions and dreams**: This shows that purity of heart and faithfulness to God come before enlightenment in divine mysteries. Daniel would later receive great revelation, but now he simply showed himself a dedicated follower of God.

c. **None was found like Daniel, Hananiah, Mishael, and Azariah**: These young men from Jerusalem were immersed in the study of Babylonian culture, literature, and religion; yet they remained faithful to God. The work of the prophets like Jeremiah, Zephaniah and Habakkuk was not in vain. They were *in* Babylon, but not *of* Babylon.

d. **Thus Daniel continued until the first year of King Cyrus**: Daniel had a long, successful career in the worst of circumstances. He worked for tyrants who thought nothing of killing their staff and advisors, much less of firing them. His employer suffered the worst kind of hostile takeover when the Medo-Persian Empire conquered the Babylonian Empire. The seeds of his great success are evident in the very first chapter of the Book of Daniel.

i. Daniel and his friends show us that inner conviction can overcome *any* outer pressure, and that God-honoring convictions yield God-given rewards.

Daniel 2 - Nebuchadnezzar Dreams of an Image

A. Nebuchadnezzar's dream.

1. (1) The troubling dream.

Now in the second year of Nebuchadnezzar's reign, Nebuchadnezzar had dreams; and his spirit was so troubled that his sleep left him.

> a. **In the second year**: It is difficult to understand the exact time this speaks of. Some commentators say this happened while Daniel was in his three-year training course; others say that it was soon after he finished.
>
> > i. The ancient Babylonians spoke of the beginning and end of the reign of their kings in a way that often overlapped years. Therefore, the year 602 B.C. could be both the second year of Nebuchadnezzar's reign and after three years of training for the Hebrew youths.
>
> b. **His spirit was so troubled that his sleep left him**: There was something disturbing about this dream and Nebuchadnezzar knew that it was unusually significant.

2. (2-9) Nebuchadnezzar demands to know the dream and its interpretation from his wise men.

Then the king gave the command to call the magicians, the astrologers, the sorcerers, and the Chaldeans to tell the king his dreams. So they came and stood before the king. And the king said to them, "I have had a dream, and my spirit is anxious to know the dream." Then the Chaldeans spoke to the king in Aramaic, "O king, live forever! Tell your servants the dream, and we will give the interpretation." The king answered and said to the Chaldeans, "My decision is firm: if you do not make known the dream to me, and its interpretation, you shall be cut in pieces, and your houses shall be made an ash heap. However, if you tell the dream and its interpretation, you shall receive from me gifts, rewards, and great honor. Therefore tell me the dream and its interpretation." They answered again and said, "Let the king tell his servants the dream, and

we will give its interpretation." The king answered and said, "I know for certain that you would gain time, because you see that my decision is firm: if you do not make known the dream to me, *there is only* one decree for you! For you have agreed to speak lying and corrupt words before me till the time has changed. Therefore tell me the dream, and I shall know that you can give me its interpretation."

a. **Make known the dream to me**: It is hard to say if Nebuchadnezzar really remembered the dream or not. Perhaps he had a general sense of it but only a vague remembrance of the details.

b. **Therefore tell me the dream, and I shall know that you can give me its interpretation**: Nebuchadnezzar couldn't know for certain that the wise men gave a correct *interpretation* of the dream. But he could test their ability to tell *what* he dreamed.

i. Despite their protests, Nebuchadnezzar didn't ask too much of these **magicians, the astrologers, the sorcerers**, and the **Chaldeans**. These men made their living on their supposed ability to contact the gods and gain secrets from the spirit realm. If they were really what they claimed to be, they should be able to tell Nebuchadnezzar *both* the dream and its interpretation.

c. **You shall be cut in pieces**: The harsh threat of Nebuchadnezzar and the method of execution he described are both perfectly consistent with the character of ancient eastern monarchs.

i. Archer described one method of dismemberment: four trees were bent inwards and tied together at the top. The victim was tied to these four trees with a rope at each limb. Then the top rope was cut and the body snapped into four pieces.

d. **The Chaldeans**: This is the first mention of the **Chaldeans** as a class of soothsayers to the king. Critics take the use of this word as a mistake that only a second century B.C. writer would make. Critics suppose that in Daniel's day, the term **Chaldean** was *only* used as a racial designation, describing what the Chaldeans thought was the master race who ruled Nebuchadnezzar's superpower empire.

i. But linguistic research has demonstrated that the Babylonian word for an astrologer-priest and their word for their supposed master race were homonyms, both having the sound **Chaldean** (*kas-du* in Babylonian), but each retaining their own meaning. This is the same way that the English sound *tu* can mean *to*, *two*, or *too*.

ii. Daniel's understanding of this is clear from the text, because he *also* used the term **Chaldean** in its racial sense (Daniel 3:8 and 5:30).

e. **Then the Chaldeans spoke to the king in Aramaic**: From Daniel 2:4 to 7:28, the Biblical text is in Aramaic - not Hebrew. This is the only section of the Bible written in Aramaic. This was the language of the Babylonian Empire.

3. (10-11) The wise men explain the impossibility of Nebuchadnezzar's request.

The Chaldeans answered the king, and said, "There is not a man on earth who can tell the king's matter; therefore no king, lord, or ruler has *ever* asked such things of any magician, astrologer, or Chaldean. *It is* a difficult thing that the king requests, and there is no other who can tell it to the king except the gods, whose dwelling is not with flesh."

a. **There is not a man on earth who can tell the king's matter**: When the Chaldeans said this they admitted that true revelation comes from God down to man. They understood - perhaps against their own inclinations - that revelation was not the *achievement* of man.

i. Despite all their wisdom - real and imagined - these wise men had no answer for Nebuchadnezzar, because only *God* could bring an answer to the king.

ii. "They were like some modern ministers of our own day who spend their time studying philosophy, psychiatry, psychology, social science, political science, and then continue under the pretense of being God's messengers to men." (Strauss)

b. **No king, lord, or ruler has ever asked such things**: The strategy of the wise men was to convince the king that he was unreasonable, not that they were incompetent.

c. **Except the gods, whose dwelling is not with flesh**: As far as these pagan magicians, astrologers, and wise men knew, this was true. They did not know what we know so plainly since the revelation of Jesus - that He is *Immanuel, God with us* (Matthew 1:23).

4. (12-13) A furious Nebuchadnezzar sentences all his wise men to death.

For this reason the king was angry and very furious, and gave a command to destroy all the wise *men* of Babylon. So the decree went out, and they began killing the wise *men;* and they sought Daniel and his companions, to kill *them.*

a. **The king was angry and very furious**: Though he was a despot, Nebuchadnezzar knew that false religion is worse than useless. He knew that it was a curse, and he had no use for wise men that could not bring him wisdom from God.

b. **Gave a command to destroy all the wise men of Babylon**: As a new king, Nebuchadnezzar also perhaps used the situation to test the suitability of his father's old advisors. The dream provided him with a good reason to clean house.

B. God reveals the dream to Daniel.

1. (14-16) Daniel reacts to Nebuchadnezzar's decree by asking for a brief extension.

Then with counsel and wisdom Daniel answered Arioch, the captain of the king's guard, who had gone out to kill the wise *men* of Babylon; he answered and said to Arioch the king's captain, "Why is the decree from the king so urgent?" Then Arioch made the decision known to Daniel. So Daniel went in and asked the king to give him time, that he might tell the king the interpretation.

a. **With counsel and wisdom Daniel answered Arioch**: Daniel was obviously innocent in all this, yet he calmly and discretely dealt with the crisis. Daniel's calmness in this crisis showed what kind of man he really was. In one sense, crises do not *make* the man. Instead, they *reveal* the man.

b. **Asked the king to give him time**: This wasn't just a stalling tactic. Daniel knew that it takes time to listen to the Lord and to wait upon Him, and Daniel was willing to take the time if the king would grant it.

2. (17-18) Daniel asks his companions for prayer.

Then Daniel went to his house, and made the decision known to Hananiah, Mishael, and Azariah, his companions, that they might seek mercies from the God of heaven concerning this secret, so that Daniel and his companions might not perish with the rest of the wise *men* of Babylon.

a. **That they might seek mercies from the God of heaven**: Daniel was in the type of situation where only God could meet his need. Therefore, he knew how important it was for both him and his companions to pray.

i. The battle was won when Daniel prayed with his friends. Praying friends are a blessing, and "In prayer meetings such as this history has been made." (Strauss)

b. **Concerning this secret**: Daniel had confidence that God could do an unprecedented miracle. Joseph had interpreted dreams with God's help, but had not reconstructed the dreams.

c. **Might not perish**: Considering what was at stake, there is little doubt that their prayers were extremely earnest. God listens to earnest prayer.

3. (19) God reveals Nebuchadnezzar's dream and its interpretation to Daniel.

Then the secret was revealed to Daniel in a night vision. So Daniel blessed the God of heaven.

a. **The secret was revealed to Daniel**: This was not *religion*, but *revelation*. Daniel did not find it out, God **revealed** it to him.

i. Christianity begins with the principle of *revelation*. What we know about God is what He has *revealed* to us. We do actively seek Him, but we seek what He has *revealed*. Our job isn't to figure things out about God, but to understand what He has revealed to us.

b. **In a night vision**: We don't know exactly what this is. It may have been a dream, or a supernatural vision that happened at night.

4. (20-23) Daniel praises God for this revelation.

Daniel answered and said:

"Blessed be the name of God forever and ever,
For wisdom and might are His.
And He changes the times and the seasons;
He removes kings and raises up kings;
He gives wisdom to the wise
And knowledge to those who have understanding.
He reveals deep and secret things;
He knows what *is* in the darkness,
And light dwells with Him.
I thank You and praise You,
O God of my fathers;
You have given me wisdom and might,
And have now made known to me what we asked of You,
For You have made known to us the king's demand."

a. **He changes... He removes... He knows**: Daniel praised God for His power and might. Daniel thought of how God is in command of all things, and how God is mightier than a mighty king like Nebuchadnezzar.

b. **He gives... He reveals**: Daniel praised God for His *communication* to man. All God's power and might were of little help to Daniel if God stayed silent. Daniel was grateful that God revealed His great knowledge.

c. **You have given... You have made known to us**: Daniel had the certainty of faith to believe that God gave him the answer, even before confirming it before Nebuchadnezzar.

i. Our level of faith is often indicated by how long it takes us to start praising God. If we won't praise Him until the answer is in hand, then we don't have much faith. Greater faith is able to praise God when the *promise* is given and received.

C. The dream of Nebuchadnezzar and its interpretation.

1. (24-30) Daniel is ushered into the king's presence, and gives glory to God for revealing the dream.

Therefore Daniel went to Arioch, whom the king had appointed to destroy the wise *men* of Babylon. He went and said thus to him: "Do not destroy the wise *men* of Babylon; take me before the king, and I will tell the king the interpretation." Then Arioch quickly brought Daniel before the king, and said thus to him, "I have found a man of the captives of Judah, who will make known to the king the interpretation." The king answered and said to Daniel, whose name *was* Belteshazzar, "Are you able to make known to me the dream which I have seen, and its interpretation?" Daniel answered in the presence of the king, and said, "The secret which the king has demanded, the wise *men*, the astrologers, the magicians, and the soothsayers cannot declare to the king. But there is a God in heaven who reveals secrets, and He has made known to King Nebuchadnezzar what will be in the latter days. Your dream, and the visions of your head upon your bed, were these: As for you, O king, thoughts came *to* your *mind while* on your bed, *about* what would come to pass after this; and He who reveals secrets has made known to you what will be. But as for me, this secret has not been revealed to me because I have more wisdom than anyone living, but for *our* sakes who make known the interpretation to the king, and that you may know the thoughts of your heart.

a. **I have a found a man**: Arioch tried to glorify himself and Daniel for the answer to the king's dream. But Daniel refused to take credit, recognizing that the credit went to God, who revealed this dream to Daniel.

b. **What will be in the latter days**: Nebuchadnezzar's dream didn't just concern himself for his kingdom, but the whole span of the future - which was to Nebuchadnezzar **the latter days**.

2. (31-35) Daniel describes Nebuchadnezzar's dream.

"You, O king, were watching; and behold, a great image! This great image, whose splendor *was* excellent, stood before you; and its form *was* awesome. This image's head *was* of fine gold, its chest and arms of silver, its belly and thighs of bronze, its legs of iron, its feet partly of iron and partly of clay. You watched while a stone was cut out without hands, which struck the image on its feet of iron and clay, and broke them in pieces. Then the iron, the clay, the bronze, the silver, and the gold were

crushed together, and became like chaff from the summer threshing floors; the wind carried them away so that no trace of them was found. And the stone that struck the image became a great mountain and filled the whole earth."

a. **Behold, a great image**: Daniel's description was clear. This was a massive and spectacular **image** made of different materials (**fine gold... silver... bronze... iron... partly of iron and partly of clay**).

i. The materials descended in value from top to bottom, with **gold** at the top and **iron** mixed with **clay** at the bottom.

b. **Broke them in pieces**: This spectacular image was destroyed by a **stone** made **without hands**, and what remained of it was blown away like worthless chaff, while the stone **became a great mountain and filled the whole earth**.

3. (36-45) The interpretation of the dream.

"**This *is* the dream. Now we will tell the interpretation of it before the king. You, O king, *are* a king of kings. For the God of heaven has given you a kingdom, power, strength, and glory; and wherever the children of men dwell, or the beasts of the field and the birds of the heaven, He has given *them* into your hand, and has made you ruler over them all; you *are* this head of gold. But after you shall arise another kingdom inferior to yours; then another, a third kingdom of bronze, which shall rule over all the earth. And the fourth kingdom shall be as strong as iron, inasmuch as iron breaks in pieces and shatters everything; and like iron that crushes, *that kingdom* will break in pieces and crush all the others. Whereas you saw the feet and toes, partly of potter's clay and partly of iron, the kingdom shall be divided; yet the strength of the iron shall be in it, just as you saw the iron mixed with ceramic clay. And *as* the toes of the feet *were* partly of iron and partly of clay, *so* the kingdom shall be partly strong and partly fragile. As you saw iron mixed with ceramic clay, they will mingle with the seed of men; but they will not adhere to one another, just as iron does not mix with clay. And in the days of these kings the God of heaven will set up a kingdom which shall never be destroyed; and the kingdom shall not be left to other people; it shall break in pieces and consume all these kingdoms, and it shall stand forever. Inasmuch as you saw that the stone was cut out of the mountain without hands, and that it broke in pieces the iron, the bronze, the clay, the silver, and the gold; the great God has made known to the king what will come to pass after this. The dream is certain, and its interpretation is sure.**"

a. **Now we will tell the interpretation**: Daniel first accurately reported the *content* of Nebuchadnezzar's dream. This gave Daniel credibility when explaining what the dream *meant*: **the interpretation**.

b. **You are this head of gold**: Nebuchadnezzar was clearly said to be the head of gold. After him would come three other kingdoms, each represented by the different materials Nebuchadnezzar saw in his dream. After the succession of kingdoms, then came the final kingdom set up by God.

> i. "Nebuchadnezzar's kingdom was likened unto gold because it was an *absolute* monarchy, God's ideal government. Nebuchadnezzar was not, however, God's ideal monarch!" (Talbot)

c. **The dream is certain, and its interpretation is sure**: This prophetic dream was clearly fulfilled in history.

> i. Three dominating empires came after Babylon: Medo-Persia, Greece, and Rome. The nature of these empires was accurately reflected by the nature of the image Nebuchadnezzar saw in his dream.

> ii. The empires succeeding Babylon were inferior to Nebuchadnezzar's **head of gold** in the sense of their centralization of absolute power. Nebuchadnezzar was an absolute monarch, and the succeeding empires were progressively less so. They were larger and lasted longer than Babylon, but none held as much centralized power as Nebuchadnezzar did.

> iii. "Babylon, the head of *gold*, was an absolute autocracy. Persia, a monarchial oligarchy with the nobles equal to the king in all but office, is represented by *silver*. Greece is set forth by *brass*, indicated the still lower value of it aristocracy of mind and influence... Rome, a democratic imperialism, with military dominion dependent upon the choice of army and citizenry and administered in the spirit of martial law, is set forth by *iron*." (Newell)

> iv. The third kingdom of bronze was the one **which shall rule over all the earth**. Indeed, Alexander's Grecian Empire was the largest among those compared in the image (except the final government of the Messiah).

> v. The Babylonian Empire stood for 66 years; the Medo-Persian Empire for 208 years; the Grecian Empire for 185 years, and the Roman Empire stood for more than 500 years.

> vi. Liberal commentators do not believe that the fourth kingdom is Rome, but they say it is Greece, and that the second and third kingdoms are Media and Persia respectively, instead of the Medo-

Persian Empire as a whole. They interpret this way because they believe it was impossible for Daniel to predict the rise of these empires.

d. In the days of these kings the God of heaven will set up a kingdom which shall never be destroyed: This described the fulfillment of this prophecy in the future. The stone cut **without hands** shatters a confederation of kings, represented by the feet of the image, and then God's Kingdom will dominate the earth.

i. Since Roman history provides no fulfillment of this federation of kings (which seems to number ten, because of the number of toes, and passages like Daniel 7:24 and Revelation 17:12) this prophecy must still be future.

ii. Since the fall of the Roman Empire, there has never been a world-dominating empire equal to Rome. Many have tried - the Huns, Islam, the so-called Holy Roman Empire, Napoleon, Hitler, Stalin - but none have succeeded. Each of these had amazing power and influence, but nothing compared to that of the Roman Empire. The Roman Empire, in some form or another, will be revived under the leadership of the final fallen dictator, the Antichrist.

iii. **It broke in pieces the iron, the bronze, the clay, the silver, and the gold**: This described a single, decisive event that shattered the image representing the glory of man's rule on earth. Since the Church or the Gospel have not, in a single decisive event, shattered the reign of human kingdoms, this event is still in the *future*.

iv. This isn't the gradual salvation of the world by the church; "Smashing is not salvation. Crushing is not conversion. Destroying is not delivering nor is pulverizing the same as purification." (Heslop)

v. This stone cut **without hands** is the Messiah, not the Church. Psalm 118:22, Isaiah 8:14, Isaiah 28:16, and Zechariah 3:9 also refer to Jesus as a stone.

vi. Therefore, the final superpower of the world is thought to be a revival of the Roman Empire, a continuation of this image. This will be the final world empire that the returning Jesus will conquer over.

e. The kingdom shall be partly strong and partly fragile: This final world empire will be according to the nature of clay mixed with iron. It will have more the *image* of true strength than the *substance* of strength.

i. As a whole, the image accurately represented human power and empire. The image *seems* invincible, but it was actually unstable at its base. Therefore one blow to the foundation could topple the whole thing.

ii. It's also significant to see that the image described *devolution*, not *evolution*. Instead of man beginning in the dust and evolving into gold, this vision declares that man's dominion begins with gold and devalues into dust.

iii. Some 40 years from this, Daniel had a vision describing the same succession of empires. Daniel saw it from God's perspective, and Nebuchadnezzar saw it from man's perspective. Nebuchadnezzar saw these empires as an impressive image; Daniel saw them as fierce beasts.

f. **The dream is certain, and its interpretation is sure**: Daniel didn't guess or analyze. Through him God announced the future. The only reason that God can predict history is because he can control it.

4. (46-49) Nebuchadnezzar's reaction to Daniel's reporting of the dream and its interpretation.

Then King Nebuchadnezzar fell on his face, prostrate before Daniel, and commanded that they should present an offering and incense to him. The king answered Daniel, and said, "Truly your God *is* the God of gods, the Lord of kings, and a revealer of secrets, since you could reveal this secret." Then the king promoted Daniel and gave him many great gifts; and he made him ruler over the whole province of Babylon, and chief administrator over all the wise *men* of Babylon. Also Daniel petitioned the king, and he set Shadrach, Meshach, and Abed-Nego over the affairs of the province of Babylon; but Daniel *sat* in the gate of the king.

a. **Nebuchadnezzar fell on his face**: This great king was obviously impressed. He wasn't in the habit of showing such respect to anyone, especially a foreign slave who was about to be executed with the rest of the wise men. This confirmed that Daniel accurately reported the dream and skillfully explained its meaning.

b. **Your God is the God of gods**: Nebuchadnezzar knew that it wasn't Daniel himself that revealed these things, but Daniel's God revealed it through Daniel. Daniel wanted the glory to go to God, and it did.

c. **The king promoted Daniel**: Daniel not only had his life spared, but he was promoted to high office - and he made sure his friends were also promoted. It was fitting that Daniel's friends got to share in his advancement, because they accomplished much of the victory through their prayers.

Daniel 3 - Saved in the Fiery Furnace

A. Nebuchadnezzar erects an image and demands everyone worship it.

1. (1) The image is made and set up.

Nebuchadnezzar the king made an image of gold, whose height *was* sixty cubits *and* its width six cubits. He set it up in the plain of Dura, in the province of Babylon.

> a. **Nebuchadnezzar the king made an image of gold**: There is considerable debate regarding when this happened. Some think it was a short time after the events of Daniel 2, but others think it happened many years later.
>
> > i. There is a discernible link between Nebuchadnezzar's dream in Daniel 2 and the image he made in Daniel 3. It seems that Nebuchadnezzar deliberately made an *entire* statue of gold, to say that the day of his reign and authority would never end - in contradiction to God's declared plan.
>
> b. **An image of gold**: The image was more like a stylized obelisk rather than a normal statue, being 90 feet (30 meters) high and 9 feet (3 meters) wide. Being so large, it is safe to say that it was not made of solid gold but probably wood overlaid with gold. This was a common method of construction in the ancient world.
>
> > i. "On the plains of Dura there stands today, a rectilinear mound, about twenty feet high, an exact square of about forty-six feet at the base, resembling the pedestal of a colossal statue." (Heslop)

2. (2-3) All Babylonia's dignitaries gathered at the dedication of the image.

And King Nebuchadnezzar sent *word* to gather together the satraps, the administrators, the governors, the counselors, the treasurers, the judges, the magistrates, and all the officials of the provinces, to come to the dedication of the image which King Nebuchadnezzar had set up. So the satraps, the administrators, the governors, the counselors,

the treasurers, the judges, the magistrates, and all the officials of the provinces gathered together for the dedication of the image that King Nebuchadnezzar had set up; and they stood before the image that Nebuchadnezzar had set up.

a. **Gather together the satraps**: **Satrap** is a Persian loan word that means *protector of the realm*. It refers to a specific category of public officials.

b. **All the officials of the provinces, to come to the dedication of the image**: The demand that all come to the dedication ceremony means that Nebuchadnezzar meant to use the worship of this image as a test of allegiance.

3. (4-6) The command to worship the image.

Then a herald cried aloud: "To you it is commanded, O peoples, nations, and languages, *that* at the time you hear the sound of the horn, flute, harp, lyre, *and* psaltery, in symphony with all kinds of music, you shall fall down and worship the gold image that King Nebuchadnezzar has set up; and whoever does not fall down and worship shall be cast immediately into the midst of a burning fiery furnace."

a. **Horn, flute, harp, lyre, and psaltery**: Some of these musical instruments are difficult to define precisely but the idea is still clear. This was an impressive orchestra.

i. The use of the Aramaic words for **lyre**, **psaltery** and **symphony** has led some critics to say that the Book of Daniel was written hundreds of years after the time of Daniel. They say this because these particular words are Aramaic words borrowed from Greek words and supposedly Daniel did not have these words at his disposal in the sixth century B.C., and they supposedly did not come into the Hebrew vocabulary until the third century B.C.

ii. Nevertheless, ancient records tell us there were Greeks in the region of Assyria, Babylon, and Persia as far back as the *eighth* century B.C. Archaeology also proves beyond a doubt that Greek mercenaries fought and made military settlements in and around Judea *before* the time of Daniel.

b. **Whoever does not fall down and worship shall be cast immediately into the midst of a burning fiery furnace**: The command was backed up by a powerful threat. Nebuchadnezzar regarded the refusal to worship the image as *treason*, not only as a religious offense.

i. In this, Nebuchadnezzar was just like many politicians who often seem willing to use religion to strengthen their grip on political power. Politicians are happy to blend together *spiritual* allegiance and *national* allegiance. An example of this was displayed in 1936 when Herr Baldur von Schirach, head of the youth program for Nazi Germany, said: "If we act as true Germans we act according to the laws of God. Whoever serves Adolf Hitler, the führer, serves Germany, and whoever serves Germany serves God."

ii. Another example comes from 1960 when the President of Ghana had a slightly larger than life-size statue of himself erected in front of the national house of Parliament. An inscription on the side of the statue read, "Seek ye first the political kingdom and all other things shall be added unto you." The statue was destroyed after a bloodless coup in 1966.

c. **A burning fiery furnace**: Nebuchadnezzar was not a man who allowed lawbreakers to go unpunished. In an ancient cuneiform writing, Nebuchadnezzar was described as so devoted to justice that "he did not rest night or day." The document also tells of a criminal guilty of a second offense who was decapitated, and afterwards a stone image of his head was displayed as a warning.

4. (7) The crowd obeys Nebuchadnezzar's command.

So at that time, when all the people heard the sound of the horn, flute, harp, *and* lyre, in symphony with all kinds of music, all the people, nations, and languages fell down *and* worshiped the gold image which King Nebuchadnezzar had set up.

a. **When all the people heard the sound**: Nebuchadnezzar's grand idolatry was accompanied by music - elaborate and well-produced music. This reminds us of the great inherent power in music, both for good and for evil.

b. **Fell down and worshiped the gold image**: According to Baldwin, this literally reads *as soon as they were hearing they were falling down.* There was total and immediate obedience to Nebuchadnezzar's command.

B. Three Hebrew men refuse the demand.

1. (8-12) Certain Chaldeans accuse the three Hebrew men.

Therefore at that time certain Chaldeans came forward and accused the Jews. They spoke and said to King Nebuchadnezzar, "O king, live forever! You, O king, have made a decree that everyone who hears the sound of the horn, flute, harp, lyre, *and* psaltery, in symphony with all kinds of music, shall fall down and worship the gold image; and whoever does not fall down and worship shall be cast into the midst of a burning fiery furnace. There are certain Jews whom you have set over the affairs of the province of Babylon: Shadrach, Meshach, and Abed-

Nego; **these men, O king, have not paid due regard to you. They do not serve your gods or worship the gold image which you have set up."**

a. **Certain Chaldeans came forward and accused the Jews**: These Chaldeans had an obvious political motivation against these Jews who were promoted to high office along with Daniel in the events recorded in the previous chapter.

b. **They do not serve your gods or worship the gold image**: Apparently their failure to worship the image was not discovered until these certain Chaldeans made it known. With so many thousands of government officials in attendance, it would be easy to overlook these three. Additionally, we see from this that the three Jewish men did not lodge a formal protest; they simply refrained from sharing in the sin of idolatry themselves.

i. Their actions were not *public* but neither were they *hidden*. These three Hebrew men must have known they would be discovered, yet they obeyed God rather than man. "You will not be able to go through life without being discovered: a lighted candle cannot be hid. There is a feeling among some good people that it will be wise to be very reticent, and hide their light under a bushel. They intend to lie low all the wartime, and come out when the palms are being distributed. They hope to travel to heaven by the back lanes, and skulk into glory in disguise. Ah me, what a degenerate set!" (Spurgeon)

2. (13-15) Nebuchadnezzar interviews the disobedient Hebrew men.

Then Nebuchadnezzar, in rage and fury, gave the command to bring Shadrach, Meshach, and Abed-Nego. So they brought these men before the king. Nebuchadnezzar spoke, saying to them, *"Is it true, Shadrach, Meshach, and Abed-Nego, that you do not serve my gods or worship the gold image which I have set up? Now if you are ready at the time you hear the sound of the horn, flute, harp, lyre, and psaltery, in symphony with all kinds of music, and you fall down and worship the image which I have made, good! But if you do not worship, you shall be cast immediately into the midst of a burning fiery furnace. And who is the god who will deliver you from my hands?"*

a. **Is it true**: To his credit, Nebuchadnezzar did not accept the accusation on hearsay. He made sure of it with a personal interview. This was an even greater test for Shadrach, Meshach, and Abed-Nego. It is one thing to make a stand for God; it is a greater thing to *stick to your stand* when pointedly asked, **"Is it true?"** Peter followed Jesus after His arrest, but he wilted and denied Jesus when asked, **"Is it true?"**

i. "If, standing before the heart-searching God at this time, you cannot say, 'It is true,' how should you act? If you cannot say that you take Christ's cross, and are willing to follow him at all hazards, then hearken to me and learn the truth. Do not make a profession at all. Do not talk about baptism or the Lord's Supper, nor of joining a church, nor of being a Christian; for if you do, you will lie against your own soul. If it be not true that you renounce the world's idols, do not profess that it is so. It is unnecessary that a man should profess to be what he is not; it is a sin of supererogation, a superfluity of naughtiness. If you cannot be true to Christ, if your coward heart is recreant to your Lord, do not profess to be his disciple, I beseech you. He that is married to the world, or flinthearted, had better return to his house, for he is of no service in this war." (Spurgeon)

b. **But if you do not worship, you shall be cast immediately into the midst of a burning fiery furnace**: Nebuchadnezzar would not tolerate losing face on such an important occasion. His pride made him declare, "You shall have no other gods than me."

i. We can imagine the enormous pressure on Shadrach, Meshach, and Abed-Nego to compromise. Everything in front of them - the king, the furnace, the music, their compatriots, their competitors - all of it conspired to convince them to compromise. Yet God was more real to them than any of those things. "Do not judge the situation by the king's threat and by the heat of the burning fiery furnace, but by the everlasting God and the eternal life which awaits you. Let not flute, harp, and sackbut fascinate you, but hearken to the music of the glorified. Men frown at you, but you can see God smiling on you, and so you are not moved." (Spurgeon)

c. **Who is the god who will deliver you from my hands?** Nebuchadnezzar thought nothing of insulting *all* gods with this statement. He is more of a *secularist* or a *humanist* than a *theist*. The god he *really* believes in is himself, not the gods of Babylon.

3. (16-18) The three Hebrew men insist they will never worship the image.

Shadrach, Meshach, and Abed-Nego answered and said to the king, "O Nebuchadnezzar, we have no need to answer you in this matter. If that *is the case*, our God whom we serve is able to deliver us from the burning fiery furnace, and He will deliver *us* from your hand, O king. But if not, let it be known to you, O king, that we do not serve your gods, nor will we worship the gold image which you have set up."

a. **We have no need to answer you:** They had **no need** to defend themselves. Their guilt in the matter was clear - they clearly would not bow down to this image.

b. **Our God whom we serve is able to deliver us:** In this, the Jewish men showed a good understanding and appreciation of God's great power. In fact, they knew that God was able to save them from both the **burning fiery furnace** and from the **hand** of Nebuchadnezzar himself.

c. **But if not:** In this, the Jewish men show they had a good understanding and appreciation of *submission* to God. They knew God's power, but they also knew that they must do what was right even if God did not do what they expect or hope Him to do.

> i. We often complain about our rights and what is fair. Often it is better to make a stand and endure our difficulty, leaving our fate in God's hands.

> ii. They did not doubt God's *ability*, but neither did they presume to know God's *will*. In this they agreed with Job: *Though He slay me, yet will I trust Him* (Job 13:15). They recognized that God's plan might be different than their desires. I have my own desires and dreams and I pray that God fulfills them. But if He doesn't, I can't turn my back on Him.

> iii. These were men who did *not* love too much. There are popular self-help books that hope to help people who seem to love too much, yet many Christians are hindered because they love too much. Remember that early Christians were not thrown to the lions because they worshipped Jesus, but because they would *not* worship the emperor.

> iv. In our day, many do love Jesus and think highly of Him - yet they are far from God because they also love and worship the world, sin, and self. *Do not love the world or the things in the world. If anyone loves the world, the love of the Father is not in him* (1 John 2:15).

d. **Let it be known to you, O king, that we do not serve your gods, nor will we worship the gold image which you have set up:** It took great faith to say this. God brought them to this place of great faith by preparing them with tests in less dramatic areas.

> i. These men stood firm when challenged to eat impure foods and they saw God bless their obedience. That gave them the courage to obey now, when the stakes were much higher.

> ii. Many fail in their obedience because they wait for something "big" to test their faith before they really start to obey God. Some fill their life with many small compromises; yet tell themselves that they will

stand firm when it really matters. Shadrach, Meshach, and Abed-Nego show us that obedience to God in small things really matters.

e. **Let it be known to you, O king**: The statement of Shadrach, Meshach, and Abed-Nego is also remarkable for what it does *not* have - any hint of an excuse. In a time of testing like this it is easy to think of a thousand excuses that seem to justify compromise.

i. They might have said, "*There is nothing to gain by resisting; wouldn't we do more good by living?*" It is easy to say, "We must live," but in reality, we all must die - so why not die making a stand for God?

ii. They might have said, "*We are in a different place; in Rome, do as the Romans do.*" Yet they knew that God has unlimited jurisdiction. We must do more than "perform" acts of religious obedience when we have an audience.

iii. They might have said, "*We will lose our jobs and our standard of living.*" Often when God blesses us, we make the blessing an idol and compromise God to keep what we have.

iv. They might have said, "*After all, we are not being called to renounce our God.*" They did not have a super-elastic conscience that said, "We are not bowing down to the idol, but only bowing down in respect for the king, or in honor of the music." Excuses like this are common but prove the principle that anything will serve as an excuse, when the heart is bent on compromise.

v. They might have said, "*Everybody else is doing it.*" Instead they cultivated brave personalities, willing to stand alone with God.

vi. They might have said, "*It is only for once, and not for very long. Ten minutes, just for the king. It is stupid to throw our lives away for ten minutes.*" These men knew that ten minutes could change an entire life. Ten minutes can chart the course for your eternity.

vii. They might have said, "*This is more than can be expected of us; God will understand just this once.*" It is true that God understands our struggle with sin - that is why He loves the sinner and made provision at the cross for freedom from the penalty, power, and presence of sin. Knowing that "God understands" should be a spur to obedience, not a license to sin.

viii. "I am glad that the three holy children were not 'careful to answer,' [the KJV has, "we are not careful to answer thee" here] or they might have fallen upon some crooked policy or lame excuse for compromise. What have we to do with consequences? It is ours to do the right, and leave results with the Lord." (Spurgeon)

C. The Hebrew men in the fiery furnace.

1. (19-23) The three men are cast violently into the furnace.

Then Nebuchadnezzar was full of fury, and the expression on his face changed toward Shadrach, Meshach, and Abed-Nego. He spoke and commanded that they heat the furnace seven times more than it was usually heated. And he commanded certain mighty men of valor who *were* in his army to bind Shadrach, Meshach, and Abed-Nego, *and* cast *them* into the burning fiery furnace. Then these men were bound in their coats, their trousers, their turbans, and their *other* garments, and were cast into the midst of the burning fiery furnace. Therefore, because the king's command was urgent, and the furnace exceedingly hot, the flame of the fire killed those men who took up Shadrach, Meshach, and Abed-Nego. And these three men, Shadrach, Meshach, and Abed-Nego, fell down bound into the midst of the burning fiery furnace.

a. **Nebuchadnezzar was full of fury**: No matter how brave Shadrach, Meshach, and Abed-Nego were, facing the **fury** of a king was still extremely intimidating. We get the feeling that prior to their statement Nebuchadnezzar spoke kindly, almost in a fatherly manner to these wayward boys. After hearing their bold challenge **the expression on his face changed**.

i. Despite the intense intimidation, the men stayed courageous in their confession of faith. Spurgeon eloquently described the horror of those who lose their courage at such times: "Remember also that by yielding to the fear of man you are demeaning yourself. There shall come a day when the man that was ashamed of Christ will himself be ashamed: he will wonder where he can hide his guilty head. Look at him! There he is! The traitor who denied his Lord! The Christ was spat upon and nailed to the cross, and this man was afraid to own him. To win the smile of a silly maid, to escape the jest of a coarse fellow, to win a few pieces of silver, to stand respectable among his fellow-men, he turned his back upon his Redeemer and sold his Lord; and now what can be said for him? Who can excuse him? The angels shun him as a man who was ashamed of the Lord of glory. He is clothed with shame and everlasting contempt. Even the lost in hell get away from him, for many of them were more honest than he. Is there such a man as this before me? I summon him in the name of the living God to answer for his cowardice! Let him come forth and own his crime, and humbly seek forgiveness at the hands of the gracious Savior." (Spurgeon)

b. **Bound in their coats... the furnace exceedingly hot**: Everything was done to make sure that the three Hebrew men were quickly and completely burned.

2. (24-25) Nebuchadnezzar sees four alive and well in the furnace.

Then King Nebuchadnezzar was astonished; and he rose in haste *and* spoke, saying to his counselors, "Did we not cast three men bound into the midst of the fire?" They answered and said to the king, "True, O king." "Look!" he answered, "I see four men loose, walking in the midst of the fire; and they are not hurt, and the form of the fourth is like the Son of God."

a. **Then King Nebuchadnezzar was astonished**: It is astonishing that anyone survived for a moment *inside* the furnace when others perished *at the door*.

i. The Septuagint says in Daniel 3:24 that Nebuchadnezzar's attention was caught when he heard the men singing praises in the furnace. We can imagine that the king had them cast into the furnace and didn't intend to look twice, believing they would be immediately consumed. As he walked away with a satisfied look on his face, he was immediately stopped by the sound of *singing* coming from the furnace. At a safe distance from the raging heat, he peered inside - and saw **four men loose, walking in the midst of the fire**.

ii. If this singing in the furnace is true, it reminds us of Paul and Silas singing in the Philippian jail (Acts 16:25).

b. **I see four men loose... and the form of the fourth is like the Son of God**: Nebuchadnezzar tells us who the fourth person was - **the Son of God**. Jesus was literally with them in the worst of their trial.

i. We don't know if Shadrach, Meshach, and Abed-Nego *knew* that the **Son of God** was with them in their fiery trial. Sometimes we are aware of Jesus' presence in our trials and sometimes we are not - but He is there nonetheless.

ii. Spurgeon observed that God's people are often in the furnace, and though there are different kinds of furnaces, they serve similar purposes in our life.

• There is the furnace that man prepares.

• There is the furnace that Satan prepares.

• There is the furnace that God prepares.

iii. God can deliver us *from* a trial, or He can miraculously sustain and strengthen us *in* a trial. Trapp quotes an English martyr who said this as he was burnt at the stake: "O ye Papists, behold ye look for miracles; here now you may see a miracle; for in this fire I feel no more pain than as if I were in a bed of down; but it is to me as a bed of roses."

c. **I see four men loose, walking in the midst of the fire**: Nebuchadnezzar also observed that the four men were *free* in the fire. The fire only burnt the ropes that bound them.

3. (26-27) The Hebrew men leave the furnace unharmed.

Then Nebuchadnezzar went near the mouth of the burning fiery furnace *and* spoke, saying, "Shadrach, Meshach, and Abed-Nego, servants of the Most High God, come out, and come *here*." Then Shadrach, Meshach, and Abed-Nego came from the midst of the fire. And the satraps, administrators, governors, and the king's counselors gathered together, and they saw these men on whose bodies the fire had no power; the hair of their head was not singed nor were their garments affected, and the smell of fire was not on them.

a. **Servants of the Most High God**: Before they were out of the furnace, Nebuchadnezzar recognized that these men served the *true* God, the God **Most High**.

b. **These men on whose bodies the fire had no power**: The trial had **no power** over these men because they were thoroughly submitted to the power and will of God. Before the time of Jesus, they knew the truth of Jesus' promise: *In the world you will have tribulation; but be of good cheer, I have overcome the world* (John 16:33).

c. **The smell of fire was not on them**: This demonstrates how complete their deliverance was.

i. This whole account illustrates - perhaps serving as a type of - the future of Israel during the Great Tribulation.

- Nebuchadnezzar is like the Antichrist, who forces the whole world into one religion of idolatry.

- Nebuchadnezzar's image is like the image described in Revelation 13, that the whole world will be commanded to worship.

- The fiery furnace is like the Great Tribulation, which will be great affliction for the Jews.

- The three Hebrew men are like Israel, who will be preserved through the tribulation.

- The executioners who perished are like those in league with the Antichrist, who Jesus will slay at His return.

- The mysteriously absent Daniel is like the church, not even present for this time of great tribulation.

D. Aftermath.

1. (28) Nebuchadnezzar acknowledges the greatness of the God of the three Hebrews.

Nebuchadnezzar spoke, saying, "Blessed be the God of Shadrach, Meshach, and Abed-Nego, who sent His Angel and delivered His servants who trusted in Him, and they have frustrated the king's word, and yielded their bodies, that they should not serve nor worship any god except their own God!"

a. **Blessed be the God of Shadrach, Meshach, and Abed-Nego**: Nebuchadnezzar gave glory to God, but he recognized that this great God is not *his* God. He was still **the God of** these three brave men.

b. **Who sent His Angel and delivered His servants who trusted in Him**: In Daniel 3:15 Nebuchadnezzar asked, "who *is* the god who will deliver you from my hands?" Now Nebuchadnezzar knew a great deal about this God.

- He is the God of the Hebrews (**the God of Shadrach, Meshach, and Abed-Nego**).
- He is the God who sends a Savior (**who sent His Angel**).
- He is the God of great power (**delivered His servants**).
- He is the God worthy of trust (**who trusted in Him**).
- He is the God worthy of full surrender (**frustrated the king's word, and yielded their bodies**).
- He is the God who demands exclusive allegiance (**that they should not serve nor worship any god except their own God**).

  i. Nebuchadnezzar knew a lot about God - but he did not yet know Him personally.

c. **Yielded their bodies**: Shadrach, Meshach, and Abed-Nego surrendered themselves *completely* to God - body, soul, and spirit. It was the kind of submission Paul wrote of in Romans 12:1: *present your bodies a living sacrifice, holy, acceptable to God, which is your reasonable service.*

  i. This whole account is a powerful illustration of the principle of Romans 12:1. We see Satan trying to make the believer bow down to his idealized image of what men and women should be. Christians must resist this with everything they have and pursue God's ideal. In this, we will fulfill Romans 12:2: *And do not be conformed to this world, but be transformed by the renewing of your mind, that you may prove what is that good and acceptable and perfect will of God.*

2. (29) Nebuchadnezzar makes a proclamation that nothing evil should be said against the God of the Hebrews.

"Therefore I make a decree that any people, nation, or language which speaks anything amiss against the God of Shadrach, Meshach, and Abed-Nego shall be cut in pieces, and their houses shall be made an ash heap; because there is no other God who can deliver like this." Then the king promoted Shadrach, Meshach, and Abed-Nego in the province of Babylon.

a. **Therefore I make a decree**: The three Hebrew men did not ask for Nebuchadnezzar to make this decree, and they probably did not want him to. Coerced worship isn't good, either towards an idol or towards the true God.

b. **There is no other God who can deliver like this**: Seeing God at work in the life of His people was an extremely effective testimony to Nebuchadnezzar.

i. Paul expressed the same idea in 2 Corinthians 3:2-3: *You are our epistle written in our hearts, known and read by all men; clearly you are an epistle of Christ, ministered by us, written not with ink but by the Spirit of the living God, not on tablets of stone but on tablets of flesh, that is, of the heart.*

Daniel 4 - The Fall and Rise of Nebuchadnezzar

A. Nebuchadnezzar's dream of the tree.

1. (1-3) The opening of Nebuchadnezzar's decree.

Nebuchadnezzar the king,

To all peoples, nations, and languages that dwell in all the earth:
Peace be multiplied to you.
I thought it good to declare the signs and wonders that the Most High
God has worked for me.
How great *are* His signs,
And how mighty His wonders!
His kingdom *is* an everlasting kingdom,
And His dominion *is* from generation to generation.

a. **Nebuchadnezzar the king**: This unique chapter is the testimony of a Gentile king and how God changed his heart. In this, Nebuchadnezzar is a good example of a *witness* (one who relates what he has seen and experienced).

b. **I thought it good to declare**: It *is* **good to declare** what God has done for us. Satan has a huge interest in keeping us unnaturally silent about **the signs and wonders that the Most High God has worked for** us.

c. **His kingdom is an everlasting kingdom**: Nebuchadnezzar was a great king, but in this chapter he recognized that God's kingdom was far greater and His dominion was completely unique because it is an **everlasting kingdom**.

2. (4-9) Only Daniel can explain the dream to Nebuchadnezzar.

I, Nebuchadnezzar, was at rest in my house, and flourishing in my palace. I saw a dream which made me afraid, and the thoughts on my bed and the visions of my head troubled me. Therefore I issued a decree to bring in all the wise *men* of Babylon before me, that they might make

known to me the interpretation of the dream. Then the magicians, the astrologers, the Chaldeans, and the soothsayers came in, and I told them the dream; but they did not make known to me its interpretation. But at last Daniel came before me (his name *is* Belteshazzar, according to the name of my god; in him *is* the Spirit of the Holy God), and I told the dream before him, *saying*: "Belteshazzar, chief of the magicians, because I know that the Spirit of the Holy God *is* in you, and no secret troubles you, explain to me the visions of my dream that I have seen, and its interpretation.

a. **Was at rest in my house, and flourishing in my palace**: Nebuchadnezzar's rest was the false peace of the ungodly. God soon shook him from his false security.

b. **I told them the dream; but they did not make known to me its interpretation**: This is not the same dream as in Daniel 2. Nebuchadnezzar readily told his counselors this dream, but they **did not** tell him what it meant. The dream was fairly easy to interpret; the wise men probably lacked *courage* more than *insight*. Nebuchadnezzar said they **did not make it known**, not that they *could not* make it known.

c. **At last Daniel came before me**: "And why 'at last'? Why was he not sooner sent for? If the soothsayers and sorcerers could have served the turn, Daniel had never been sought to. This is the guise of graceless men; they run not to God till all other refuges fail them." (Trapp)

d. **His name is Belteshazzar, according to the name of my god**: Before Daniel interpreted the dream described in this chapter for Nebuchadnezzar, the king of Babylon considered the Babylonian deity *Bel* his god.

i. This means that what he saw previously with Daniel and the three Hebrew young men was enough to impress him, but not enough to convert him. Being impressed with God isn't the same as being converted.

3. (10-17) The content of the dream: the rise and fall of a great tree.

These *were* the visions of my head *while* on my bed:

I was looking, and behold,
A tree in the midst of the earth,
And its height was great.
The tree grew and became strong;
Its height reached to the heavens,
And it could be seen to the ends of all the earth.
Its leaves *were* lovely,
Its fruit abundant,

And in it *was* food for all.
The beasts of the field found shade under it,
The birds of the heavens dwelt in its branches,
And all flesh was fed from it.

"I saw in the visions of my head *while* on my bed, and there was a watcher, a holy one, coming down from heaven. He cried aloud and said thus:

'Chop down the tree and cut off its branches,
Strip off its leaves and scatter its fruit.
Let the beasts get out from under it,
And the birds from its branches.
Nevertheless leave the stump and roots in the earth,
Bound with a band of iron and bronze,
In the tender grass of the field.
Let it be wet with the dew of heaven,
And *let* him graze with the beasts
On the grass of the earth.
Let his heart be changed from *that of* a man,
Let him be given the heart of a beast,
And let seven times pass over him.
'This decision *is* by the decree of the watchers,
And the sentence by the word of the holy ones,
In order that the living may know
That the Most High rules in the kingdom of men,
Gives it to whomever He will,
And sets over it the lowest of men.'

a. **A tree in the midst of the earth**: The **tree** in Nebuchadnezzar's dream was noted for its size, strength, prominence, beauty, fruit, and shelter.

b. **He cried aloud and said thus**: The **watcher** (presumably an angel) explained the fate of the tree. He noted that the tree was to be chopped down, and it would lose its size, strength, prominence, beauty, fruit, and shelter. He also said that the **tree** represented **a man** who would be **changed** and **given the heart of a beast**.

i. **Bound with a band of iron and bronze**: These were either for the tree stump's confinement or protection. The tree would no longer be free and great.

c. **In order that the living may know that the Most High rules in the kingdom of men**: Nebuchadnezzar heard these words in his dream. In light of this, the dream wasn't hard to interpret - it clearly dealt with the humbling of a great king. No wonder none of Nebuchadnezzar's counselors wanted to interpret the dream for him.

> i. Like most kings - ancient and modern - Nebuchadnezzar wanted to believe that *he* ruled instead of God or anyone else. "Both the Assyrian and the Babylonian kings thought of themselves as rulers over all the earth, so describing themselves in their inscriptions." (Wood)

4. (18) Nebuchadnezzar asks Daniel to interpret the dream.

"This dream I, King Nebuchadnezzar, have seen. Now you, Belteshazzar, declare its interpretation, since all the wise *men* of my kingdom are not able to make known to me the interpretation; but you *are* able, for the Spirit of the Holy God *is* in you."

> a. **Declare its interpretation**: Nebuchadnezzar knew he could get an honest answer from Daniel, even when the truth was hard to bear.

> b. **You are able, for the Spirit of the Holy God is in you**: Though Nebuchadnezzar recognized Daniel as a man filled with **the Spirit of the Holy God**, Nebuchadnezzar had not yet yielded himself to the Holy God.

B. Daniel's explanation of Nebuchadnezzar's dream.

1. (19-26) Daniel explains the rise and coming fall of Nebuchadnezzar.

Then Daniel, whose name was Belteshazzar, was astonished for a time, and his thoughts troubled him. *So* the king spoke, and said, "Belteshazzar, do not let the dream or its interpretation trouble you." Belteshazzar answered and said, "My lord, *may* the dream concern those who hate you, and its interpretation concern your enemies! The tree that you saw, which grew and became strong, whose height reached to the heavens and which *could be seen* by all the earth, whose leaves *were* lovely and its fruit abundant, in which *was* food for all, under which the beasts of the field dwelt, and in whose branches the birds of the heaven had their home; it *is* you, O king, who have grown and become strong; for your greatness has grown and reaches to the heavens, and your dominion to the end of the earth. And inasmuch as the king saw a watcher, a holy one, coming down from heaven and saying, 'Chop down the tree and destroy it, but leave its stump and roots in the earth, *bound* with a band of iron and bronze in the tender grass of the field; let it be wet with the dew of heaven, and let him graze with the beasts of the field, till seven times pass over him'; this is the interpretation, O king, and this is the decree of the Most High, which has come upon my lord the king: They shall drive you from men, your dwelling shall be with the beasts of the field, and they shall make you eat grass like oxen. They shall wet you with the dew of heaven, and seven times shall pass over you, till you

know that the Most High rules in the kingdom of men, and gives it to whomever He chooses. And inasmuch as they gave the command to leave the stump *and* roots of the tree, your kingdom shall be assured to you, after you come to know that Heaven rules."

a. **His thoughts troubled him**: Daniel genuinely cared for Nebuchadnezzar and was clearly affected by the meaning of the dream. He didn't *want* it to be true of his friend Nebuchadnezzar.

b. **It is you, O king**: Daniel applied the point without ambiguity. Instead of reaching for a general point (such as saying, "We all could use a little more humility") Daniel brought the truth in love. This was similar to what the prophet Nathan said to King David: *You are the man!* (2 Samuel 12:7).

i. "Great men and princes are often represented, in the language of the prophets, under the similitude of *trees*, see Ezekiel 17:5-6; 31:3 and following; Jeremiah 22:15; Psalm 1:3; 37:35." (Clarke)

c. **Drive you from men... make you eat grass like oxen... wet you with the dew of heaven**: When Daniel explained this to Nebuchadnezzar, the king probably couldn't guess just how literally it would be fulfilled.

d. **After you come to know that Heaven rules**: This was God's intended purpose for Nebuchadnezzar. The king could have avoided this humiliating fate if he genuinely humbled himself.

2. (27) Daniel, a good preacher, presses home the application: repent; perhaps it is not too late.

Therefore, O king, let my advice be acceptable to you; break off your sins by *being* righteous, and your iniquities by showing mercy to *the* poor. Perhaps there may be a lengthening of your prosperity.

a. **Break off your sins**: The right reaction to the threat of judgment is a humble repentance. Unfortunately, Nebuchadnezzar did not do this. He should have followed the example of the repentance of Nineveh at the preaching of Jonah (Jonah 3).

i. We might think that Nebuchadnezzar had more reason than most to be proud - after all, he was a great king. Still, he should have remembered the principle Benjamin Franklin put forth in one of his proverbs: "The greatest monarch on the proudest throne, is obliged to sit upon his own rear end."

b. **Break off your sins by being righteous, and your iniquities by showing mercy to the poor**: Nebuchadnezzar was not only counseled to *stop* sinning, but also to *practice* righteousness and generosity.

C. Fulfillment of the dream.

1. (28-33) Nebuchadnezzar is stricken with madness, and humbled.

All *this* came upon King Nebuchadnezzar. At the end of the twelve months he was walking about the royal palace of Babylon. The king spoke, saying, "Is not this great Babylon, that I have built for a royal dwelling by my mighty power and for the honor of my majesty?" While the word *was still* in the king's mouth, a voice fell from heaven: "King Nebuchadnezzar, to you it is spoken: the kingdom has departed from you! And they shall drive you from men, and your dwelling *shall be* with the beasts of the field. They shall make you eat grass like oxen; and seven times shall pass over you, until you know that the Most High rules in the kingdom of men, and gives it to whomever He chooses." That very hour the word was fulfilled concerning Nebuchadnezzar; he was driven from men and ate grass like oxen; his body was wet with the dew of heaven till his hair had grown like eagles' *feathers* and his nails like birds' *claws*.

a. **At the end of the twelve months**: God gave Nebuchadnezzar twelve months to repent, and he probably forgot about the dream during that time - but God didn't forget.

b. **Is not this great Babylon**: Babylon was truly one of the spectacular cities of the ancient world, which included the famous hanging gardens built by Nebuchadnezzar.

> i. Daniel knew that the new Babylon was the creation of Nebuchadnezzar (Daniel 4:30), something previously thought untrue and only verified by recent archaeology. Nobody in the Maccabean period (second century B.C.) thought Nebuchadnezzar had built the new Babylon.

> ii. In the British Museum, there are six columns of writing recovered from Babylon with describe the huge building projects of Nebuchadnezzar and his zeal to enlarge and beautify the city.

> iii. Most of the bricks found in the excavations of Babylon carry this stamp: "Nebuchadnezzar, king of Babylon, supporter of Esagila and Ezida, exalted first-born son of Nabopolassar, king of Babylon."

> iv. Late-daters of Daniel (who say that it was written in the times of the Macabees, around 167 B.C.) can't explain how a late writer would know to accurately attribute the spectacular buildings of Babylon to Nebuchadnezzar. One liberal Bible commentator, R. H. Pfeiffer, said of this problem: "We shall presumably never know."

c. **They shall drive you from men... eat grass like oxen**: The announcement came to Nebuchadnezzar in the same words he heard in his dream. This showed him that the dream was about to be fulfilled, and he would be reduced to the existence of an animal - specifically, an ox.

> i. The form of insanity in which men think of themselves as animals and imitate the behavior of an animal has been observed. Some call it generally *insania zoanthropica* and more specifically in Nebuchadnezzar's case, *boanthropy*, the delusion that one is an ox.

> ii. Walvoord quotes a Dr. Raymond Harrison of Britain, who in 1946 had a patient suffering from boanthropy, just as Nebuchadnezzar suffered.

d. **He was driven from men and ate grass like oxen**: There is no corresponding record of this seven-year (**seven times**) period of insanity in the secular historical records of Babylon - exactly as we would expect, considering the customs of that time. Nevertheless, Abydenus, a Greek historian, wrote in 268 B.C. that Nebuchadnezzar was "possessed by some god" and that he had "immediately disappeared." (Wood)

> i. Some dismiss this account of Nebuchadnezzar's madness as unhistorical, but there is no historical record of his governmental activity between 582 B.C. and 575 B.C. This silence is deafening, especially when we keep in mind how Near Eastern leaders liked to egotistically trumpet their achievements - and hide their embarrassments.

> ii. "Although critics have imagined a series of incredible objections to accepting this chapter as authentic and reasonably accurate, the narrative actually reads very sensibly and the objections seem trivial and unsupported." (Walvoord)

> iii. Nebuchadnezzar was given the opportunity to humble himself, and he did not. Now God humbled him, and the experience was much more severe than it would have been had Nebuchadnezzar humbled himself.

2. (34-37) A repentant Nebuchadnezzar is restored, and praises God.

And at the end of the time I, Nebuchadnezzar, lifted my eyes to heaven, and my understanding returned to me; and I blessed the Most High and praised and honored Him who lives forever:

For His dominion *is* an everlasting dominion,
And His kingdom *is* from generation to generation.
All the inhabitants of the earth *are* reputed as nothing;
He does according to His will in the army of heaven
And *among* the inhabitants of the earth.
No one can restrain His hand
Or say to Him, "What have You done?"

At the same time my reason returned to me, and for the glory of my kingdom, my honor and splendor returned to me. My counselors and nobles resorted to me, I was restored to my kingdom, and excellent majesty was added to me. Now I, Nebuchadnezzar, praise and extol and honor the King of heaven, all of whose works *are* truth, and His ways justice. And those who walk in pride He is able to put down.

a. **At the end of the time**: Nebuchadnezzar could not break free from his madness until God appointed the **end of the time**. Then he had the opportunity to humble himself and lift **his eyes to heaven**.

i. Nebuchadnezzar knew the principle Spurgeon later explained: "The God whom we serve not only exists, but reigns. No other position would become him but that of unlimited sovereignty over all his creatures."

b. **I blessed the Most High and praised and honored Him**: Nebuchadnezzar could only see the truth about *himself* when he first saw the truth about *God*. The Babylonian King did see who God was, and he eloquently praised His sovereignty. *After* this his **reason returned**.

i. This return of reason results in *worship*. "We do not worship enough, my brethren. Even in our public gatherings we do not have enough worship. O worship the King! Bow your heads now - bow your spirits rather, and adore him that liveth for ever and ever. Your thoughts, your emotions, these are better than bullocks and he-goats to be offered on the altar: God will accept them. Worship him with lowliest reverence, for you are nothing, and he is all in all." (Spurgeon)

ii. This return of reason results in *prayer*. If we believe what Nebuchadnezzar believed about God, it will certainly show in our prayer life. We will know that God can change the heart and mind of man, the course of rivers, the flow of the oceans, the distribution of resources, and the assignment of angels.

iii. Spurgeon suggested the proper response of the believer to the greatness and sovereignty of God:

- Have a heart of humble adoration.
- Show a heart of unquestioning acceptance.
- Exercise the spirit of reverent love.
- Let your spirit have profound delight.

c. **I was restored to my kingdom, and excellent majesty was added to me**: God *wanted* to restore Nebuchadnezzar. The goal wasn't to bring him low, but to bring him to his proper place before God and among men.

Truly, Nebuchadnezzar learned that **those who walk in pride He is able to put down**.

i. The abiding lesson is plain: *God resists the proud but gives grace to the humble* (James 4:6). There have been many who rise from humble origins to great glory, and then fall. Perhaps it is better to have never been raised up than to rise and then fall. Most, if not all, fall through pride; and a *proud look* is number one on the list of God's most hated sins (Proverbs 6:16-19).

ii. We also see that God *will* glorify himself among the nations. When Nebuchadnezzar took some of the treasures of the Jerusalem temple and put them in the temples of his gods, he had reason to believe that his gods were stronger than the God of Abraham, Isaac and Jacob. By the end of Daniel 4, Nebuchadnezzar knew which God was the true God. And when Nebuchadnezzar knew it, he wasn't shy about telling people what he had learned - he was a true witness, giving testimony to God's great works.

iii. Some find prophetic significance in this account. Since Babylon is used in the Scriptures as a figure of the world system in general, we can say:

- Nebuchadnezzar's madness foreshadows the madness of Gentile nations in their rejection of God.
- Nebuchadnezzar's fall typifies Jesus' judgment of the nations.
- Nebuchadnezzar's restoration foreshadows the restoring of some of these nations in the millennial kingdom.

Daniel 5 - The Writing on the Wall

A. A disturbing message from God.

1. (1-4) Belshazzar's great, blasphemous feast.

Belshazzar the king made a great feast for a thousand of his lords, and drank wine in the presence of the thousand. While he tasted the wine, Belshazzar gave the command to bring the gold and silver vessels which his father Nebuchadnezzar had taken from the temple which *had been* in Jerusalem, that the king and his lords, his wives, and his concubines might drink from them. Then they brought the gold vessels that had been taken from the temple of the house of God which *had been* in Jerusalem; and the king and his lords, his wives, and his concubines drank from them. They drank wine, and praised the gods of gold and silver, bronze and iron, wood and stone.

a. **Belshazzar the king**: When we come to Daniel 5, Nebuchadnezzar is no longer the king of Babylon. How did it pass from Nebuchadnezzar to **Belshazzar**? The ancient historian Berosus gives us the following order of events:

- Nebuchadnezzar died after a 43-year reign.

- His son, Evil-Merodach (described in 2 Kings 25:27-30 and Jeremiah 52:31-34) ruled for only two years when he was assassinated by his brother-in-law Neriglassar, because his rule was arbitrary and licentious.

- Neriglassar (mentioned as Nergalsharezer in Jeremiah 39:3, 13) ruled for four years until he died a natural death.

- His son, Laborosoarchod, only a child and of diminished mental capacity, ruled for only nine months when he was beaten to death by a gang of conspirators.

- The conspirators appointed Nabonidus, one of their gang, to be king. He ruled until Cyrus the Persian conquered Babylon.

b. **Belshazzar the king**: For a long time, historians and archaeologists knew that Nabonidus was said to be the last king of Babylon, not **Belshazzar** (who was Nabonidus' eldest son). The solution to this so-called discrepancy was apparent when evidence was uncovered indicating not only Belshazzar's association with Nabonidus on the throne, but also demonstrating that during the last part of his reign Nabonidus lived in Arabia and left the conduct of the Kingdom of Babylon to his eldest son **Belshazzar**.

i. There was no additional mention of **Belshazzar**, the eldest son and co-regent with Nabonidus, until the *Nabonidus Cylinder* was discovered in this century. It is now displayed in the British Museum.

ii. According to Babylonian records, Belshazzar became co-regent in the third year of Nabonidus' reign (553 B.C.) and continued in that capacity till the fall of Babylon (539 B.C.).

iii. It is most likely that at the time of Daniel 5, Nabonidus had gone out to fight the Medo-Persian army and had been already captured. Those armies now surrounded Babylon, and were looking for a way into the strongly defended city.

c. **Made a great feast for a thousand of his lords**: Belshazzar was not afraid of the siege surrounding the city. He was confident because of Babylon's impressive defenses and his vast supplies.

i. Conservative calculations set the dimensions of the ancient city of Babylon like this:

- The outer walls were 17 miles (27 kilometers) long.
- These walls were 22 feet (7 meters) thick and 90 feet (28 meters) high.
- The outer walls also had guard towers another 100 feet (30 meters) high.
- The city gates were made of bronze.
- A system of inner and outer walls and moats made the city very secure.

d. **Which his father Nebuchadnezzar had taken from the temple**: Nebuchadnezzar was not the direct father of Belshazzar. Either Nebuchadnezzar was his grandfather through his mother's side, or he was Belshazzar's father in the sense of having previously occupied the throne Belshazzar now sat on. Either usage of the term **father** was accepted in ancient times.

e. **They drank wine, and praised the gods of gold and silver, bronze and iron, wood and stone**: The scene of partying while a hostile army surrounded the city reminds us of the spirit of our present age. Many today have the idea that the best response to the seeming danger of the times is to forget about it and escape into the pursuit of pleasure.

i. In Ephesians 5:18 Paul calls drunkenness *dissipation*; drunkenness is a *waste* of resources that should be submitted to Jesus. John Trapp wrote of drinking "all the three outs" – "that is, ale out of the pot, money out of the purse, and wit out of the head." (Trapp's commentary on Galatians 5:21)

f. **They brought the gold vessels that had been taken from the temple of the house of God which had been in Jerusalem**: Belshazzar was foolish enough to not only lose all semblance of self-control at this party, but also to openly mock God. He committed the sin of *sacrilege*, something few people are concerned with today.

i. Gathering the vessels from the Jewish temple served the purpose of reminding the partiers of a previous victory, and Belshazzar hoped it would boost morale. "As if these dung-hill deities had mastered and spoiled the God of Israel... This was blasphemy in a high degree, and therefore presently punished by God." (Trapp)

ii. In Babylon, a large court - 56 by 170 feet - has been unearthed, decorated with Greek columns. This is probably where the feast of Daniel 5 took place.

2. (5) God writes a message on a wall.

In the same hour the fingers of a man's hand appeared and wrote opposite the lampstand on the plaster of the wall of the king's palace; and the king saw the part of the hand that wrote.

a. **The fingers of a man's hand appeared**: God can and sometimes does communicate to man in unexpected and even shocking ways. Here, a hand mysteriously appeared and wrote on a wall.

b. **The king saw the part of the hand that wrote**: This, of course, is where we get the proverbial phrase *the writing on the wall*.

3. (6-9) Belshazzar's reaction to the message, and his call for someone to interpret the message.

Then the king's countenance changed, and his thoughts troubled him, so that the joints of his hips were loosened and his knees knocked against each other. The king cried aloud to bring in the astrologers, the Chaldeans, and the soothsayers. The king spoke, saying to the wise *men* of Babylon, "Whoever reads this writing, and tells me its interpretation, shall be clothed with purple and *have* a chain of gold around his neck;

and he shall be the third ruler in the kingdom." Now all the king's wise **men came, but they could not read the writing, or make known to the** **king its interpretation. Then King Belshazzar was greatly troubled, his** **countenance was changed, and his lords were astonished.**

a. **The joints of his hips were loosed and his knees knocked**: Daniel's vivid description shows us that Belshazzar was terrified. His carefree partying was so shallow that it turned from merry to terrified in a moment. This shows that his conscience was active beneath his energetic partying.

i. After all, if Belshazzar could not *understand* the writing, why should it trouble him so? It troubled him because his own conscience testified against him.

ii. "The writing on the wall he could neither read nor understand; but his conscience had written bitter things against him, which now being held to the fire of God's wrath become legible." (Trapp)

b. **Whoever reads the writing, and tells me its interpretation**: "For the king the difficulty was not to give the 'dictionary definition' of the terms, but to see what significance they had for him." (Baldwin)

c. **He shall be the third ruler in the kingdom**: Archaeologists have discovered why Belshazzar offered the interpreter of the dream the **third** place in the kingdom. The real king was Nabonidus, and his son Belshazzar ruled as *second* in the kingdom. Belshazzar couldn't give away the second place in the kingdom, because *he* was the second in the kingdom at the time. The best he had to offer was the **third** place.

d. **They could not read the writing, or make known to the king its interpretation**: When Daniel came to interpret these words, it does not seem so hard to figure out. It may be that God deliberately put a veil over the minds of these men so Daniel would be called. Others - such as Adam Clarke - suppose that the Babylonian wise men could not read the writing because it was in Hebrew.

4. (10-12) Daniel is recommended as an interpreter of the message.

The queen, because of the words of the king and his lords, came to the **banquet hall. The queen spoke, saying, "O king, live forever! Do not** **let your thoughts trouble you, nor let your countenance change. There** **is a man in your kingdom in whom *is* the Spirit of the Holy God. And** **in the days of your father, light and understanding and wisdom, like** **the wisdom of the gods, were found in him; and King Nebuchadnezzar** **your father - your father the king - made him chief of the magicians,** **astrologers, Chaldeans, *and* soothsayers. Inasmuch as an excellent** **spirit, knowledge, understanding, interpreting dreams, solving riddles,**

and explaining enigmas were found in this Daniel, whom the king named Belteshazzar, now let Daniel be called, and he will give the interpretation."

a. **The queen... came to the banquet hall**: This **queen** (or queen mother) is hard to identify with certainty. Probably it was Belshazzar's mother, the daughter of Nebuchadnezzar.

b. **There is a man in your kingdom**: When the wise men were called to explain the writing on the wall to Belshazzar, Daniel apparently was not called. It seems that Daniel was semi-retired, still holding a government office yet not a main figure in the administration.

c. **This Daniel, whom the king named Belteshazzar**: The queen referred to Daniel by his Jewish name, thus showing respect for his faith and background.

5. (13-16) Belshazzar asks Daniel to interpret the message.

Then Daniel was brought in before the king. The king spoke, and said to Daniel, "Are you that Daniel who is one of the captives from Judah, whom my father the king brought from Judah? I have heard of you, that the Spirit of God is in you, and that light and understanding and excellent wisdom are found in you. Now the wise men, the astrologers, have been brought in before me, that they should read this writing and make known to me its interpretation, but they could not give the interpretation of the thing. And I have heard of you, that you can give interpretations and explain enigmas. Now if you can read the writing and make known to me its interpretation, you shall be clothed with purple and have a chain of gold around your neck, and shall be the third ruler in the kingdom."

a. **Then Daniel was brought in before the king**: When everything seems great - when the party is going non-stop - God and His servants are mocked, neglected, and hidden away. But when the hand of heaven wrote a sobering message, panic-stricken worldlings cried out for the one who had the Spirit of God.

b. **I have heard of you**: Since Belshazzar didn't think to call for Daniel himself, it seems that his remembrance of Daniel was either long ago or just now by the queen.

i. "This silly and shallow prince hath nothing to say but what was put into his mouth by his wiser grandmother." (Trapp)

B. What the message meant.

1. (17-23) Introduction: Daniel describes Belshazzar's sinful pride.

Then Daniel answered, and said before the king, "Let your gifts be for yourself, and give your rewards to another; yet I will read the writing to the king, and make known to him the interpretation. O king, the Most High God gave Nebuchadnezzar your father a kingdom and majesty, glory and honor. And because of the majesty that He gave him, all peoples, nations, and languages trembled and feared before him. Whomever he wished, he executed; whomever he wished, he kept alive; whomever he wished, he set up; and whomever he wished, he put down. But when his heart was lifted up, and his spirit was hardened in pride, he was deposed from his kingly throne, and they took his glory from him. Then he was driven from the sons of men, his heart was made like the beasts, and his dwelling *was* with the wild donkeys. They fed him with grass like oxen, and his body was wet with the dew of heaven, till he knew that the Most High God rules in the kingdom of men, and appoints over it whomever He chooses. But you his son, Belshazzar, have not humbled your heart, although you knew all this. And you have lifted yourself up against the Lord of heaven. They have brought the vessels of His house before you, and you and your lords, your wives and your concubines, have drunk wine from them. And you have praised the gods of silver and gold, bronze and iron, wood and stone, which do not see or hear or know; and the God who *holds* your breath in His hand and owns all your ways, you have not glorified."

a. **Let your gifts be for yourself**: Remember that Daniel was troubled when he had to give Nebuchadnezzar bad news (Daniel 4:19). This wasn't the case here. Daniel was not impressed with this successor of Nebuchadnezzar.

b. **You his son, Belshazzar, have not humbled your heart, although you knew all this**: Daniel was so harsh because Belshazzar should have known better. Even if he was not raised in a godly home, Romans 1 reminds us that all men know of God through creation. Belshazzar should have known even more through God's dealings with and through Daniel. We are all responsible to honor God according to what revelation we have.

c. **The God who holds your breath in His hand and owns all your ways, you have not glorified**: It would be easy for Belshazzar to think that he never did anything against the God of Israel - at least nothing *too bad*. Yet at the very least, he had **not glorified** the true God, and every creature is obligated to give glory to their Creator.

i. The **breath** of the creature should praise the Creator, but Belshazzar blasphemed God with his breath. The **ways** of the creature should glorify the Creator, but Belshazzar used his **ways** to mock and offend God. Every creature owes something to the Creator.

ii. "If God held Belshazzar responsible, my friend, for the ray of light which shone across *his* pathway, what will He say to men living in the blaze of light which illuminates the world today? Every unconverted man in this country has more light than Belshazzar had." (Talbot)

2. (24-28) Daniel tells Belshazzar that God's judgment is at the door.

"Then the fingers of the hand were sent from Him, and this writing was written. And this is the inscription that was written:

MENE, MENE, TEKEL, UPHARSIN.

This *is* the interpretation of *each* word. MENE: God has numbered your kingdom, and finished it; TEKEL: You have been weighed in the balances, and found wanting; PERES: Your kingdom has been divided, and given to the Medes and Persians."

a. **MENE, MENE, TEKEL, UPHARSIN. This is the interpretation of each word**: "It should be observed, that *each word* stands for a *short sentence*; *mene* signifies NUMERATION; *tekel*, WEIGHING; and *peres*, DIVISION." (Clarke)

- God had Belshazzar's *number*, and it fell short.

- God *weighed* Belshazzar, and he came up light.

- God would therefore *divide* Belshazzar's kingdom to the Medes and the Persians.

b. **Weighed in the balances, and found wanting**: A mighty army and brilliant tactics overcame the Babylonian Empire, yet it still *fell from within*. The armies of the Medes and Persians could only conquer because Belshazzar and his kingdom were found lacking in spiritual and moral values.

c. **Given to the Medes and Persians**: The ancient Greek historian Herodotus relates that the Persian King Cyrus conquered Babylon by diverting the flow of the Euphrates into a nearby swamp. This lowered the level of the river so his troops marched through the water and under the river-gates. They still would not have been able to enter *had not the bronze gates of the inner walls been left inexplicably unlocked*. This was exactly what God predicted in Isaiah 44:28-45:7 and Jeremiah 51:57-58. *God opened the gates of the city of Babylon for Cyrus*, and put it in writing 200 years before it happened.

i. "In October 539 BC, Cyrus advanced into lower Mesopotamia and, leaving Babylon till last, conquered and occupied the surrounding territory. Seeing which way the wind was blowing, Nabonidus of Babylon deserted his city, leaving it in the charge of his son Belshazzar...

the taking of Babylon was as bloodless and effortless as Daniel 5 implies." (Motyer, in his commentary on Isaiah)

ii. The fall of mystery Babylon will be like the fall of real Babylon - sudden, sure, and in the midst of her worst blasphemies. "Empires do not stand by human might, man-made machines and missiles. There is not a wall high enough nor thick enough to prevent a nation from falling when God pronounces that nation's doom." (Strauss)

3. (29) Daniel is promoted.

Then Belshazzar gave the command, and they clothed Daniel with purple and *put* a chain of gold around his neck, and made a proclamation concerning him that he should be the third ruler in the kingdom.

a. **They clothed Daniel with purple**: Though his words were harsh, Daniel was quickly rewarded. Either Belshazzar knew that Daniel was right and bravely tried to do the best under the inevitable circumstances, or he disbelieved the whole thing and promoted Daniel in a display of big-hearted fun.

b. **That he should be the third ruler in the kingdom**: Daniel held this post for only a few hours. This shows how temporary the awards and accolades of this world are. In the kingdom that succeeded Belshazzar Daniel was also promoted, but that was due to God, not to Belshazzar.

4. (30-31) The death of Belshazzar and the rise of Darius the Mede.

That very night Belshazzar, king of the Chaldeans, was slain. And Darius the Mede received the kingdom, *being* about sixty-two years old.

a. **That very night**: The word was fulfilled just as Daniel said. God's Word is always reliable and true.

b. **Darius the Mede received the kingdom**: Darius was a sub-king under Cyrus the Persian. He is referred to in secular history as Gubaru.

Daniel 6 - In the Lion's Den

This has long been a beloved Bible story - and no wonder. There are so many dramatic features in this story - the jealousy of political subordinates, the vanity of a king, the integrity of a man, the power and preservation of God, even wild animals and violence.

A. How Daniel was condemned to the lion's den.

1. (1-3) Daniel in the government of Darius.

It pleased Darius to set over the kingdom one hundred and twenty satraps, to be over the whole kingdom; and over these, three governors, of whom Daniel *was* one, that the satraps might give account to them, so that the king would suffer no loss. Then this Daniel distinguished himself above the governors and satraps, because an excellent spirit *was* in him; and the king gave thought to setting him over the whole realm.

a. **It pleased Darius**: Secular history of this period has no record of a ruler named **Darius** in the particular period and place recorded in Daniel 6. There are three possible explanations for the Darius of Daniel 6.

i. It may be that **Darius** was simply another name for Cyrus, who ruled the Medo-Persian Empire during this period.

ii. It may be that **Darius** was actually Cambyses, son of Cyrus, who served under his father as a ruler of Babylon and later inherited the throne of the entire empire.

iii. It may be that **Darius** was an ancient official known as *Gubaru* in ancient documents, whom Cyrus appointed as ruler over Babylon immediately after its capture. It is the opinion of this commentator that this *Gubaru* was the same person as **Darius**. In fact, "Darius" may be an honorific title meaning, "holder of the scepter."

iv. Ancient documents show that the man Gubaru had the power to make appointments, to assemble an army, to levy taxes, and to possess palaces. Gubaru was in a very real sense the king over Babylon.

b. **Daniel distinguished himself**: Daniel was one of three leaders directly under Darius, and he shined above the other two leaders because he had **an excellent spirit**. Daniel had a good attitude in his work and life, and this made him the object of attack.

2. (4-9) A plot against Daniel is conceived and initiated.

So the governors and satraps sought to find *some* **charge against Daniel concerning the kingdom; but they could find no charge or fault, because he** *was* **faithful; nor was there any error or fault found in him. Then these men said, "We shall not find any charge against this Daniel unless we find** *it* **against him concerning the law of his God." So these governors and satraps thronged before the king, and said thus to him: "King Darius, live forever! All the governors of the kingdom, the administrators and satraps, the counselors and advisors, have consulted together to establish a royal statute and to make a firm decree, that whoever petitions any god or man for thirty days, except you, O king, shall be cast into the den of lions. Now, O king, establish the decree and sign the writing, so that it cannot be changed, according to the law of the Medes and Persians, which does not alter." Therefore King Darius signed the written decree.**

a. **They could find no charge or fault, because he was faithful**: Daniel was such a **faithful** man that those who looked for a flaw in his actions or his character came up empty.

i. Sometimes today a candidate or nominee for political office is set under this kind of scrutiny, but imagine looking as hard as you can at a public servant in office some 50 years and finding *nothing wrong*. No fraudulent expense accounts. No intern scandals. No questionable business deals. No gifts from lobbyists. No accusations from his staff.

ii. Simply, there were no skeletons in Daniel's closet. His enemies examined his life and found nothing to attack - so they had to *make up* something.

b. **Nor was there any error or fault found in him**: This wasn't to imply that Daniel was actually sinless, but that he was a man of great integrity. We could also say that Daniel was especially blameless in the conduct of his professional life.

i. When he considered Daniel's integrity, Spurgeon bemoaned our modern compromises: "As for Lord Fair-Speech, Lord Time-Server,

Mr. Smooth-Man, Mr. Anything, Mr. Facing-both-Ways, Mr. Two-Tongues, and all the members of their club, Mr. By-Ends included, the entire company of them will be swept away when the Judge comes with the besom of destruction." (Spurgeon)

ii. "Daniel here is not the herald of his own virtue, but the Spirit speaks through his mouth." (Calvin)

c. **We shall not find any charge against this Daniel unless we find it against him concerning the law of his God**: These men knew Daniel well. They knew he could not be trapped into evil, but they also knew that he would be faithful to **his God** in all circumstances. Every Christian should consider if others could say the same about them.

i. The world may not know the details of doctrine or the intimacies of worship with God, but they can tell a bad temper, selfishness, conceitedness, or dishonesty when they see it. "The world is a very poor critic of my Christianity, but it is a very sufficient one of my conduct." (Maclaren)

d. **Whoever petitions any god or man for thirty days, except you, O king**: If the enemies of Daniel knew him, they also knew Darius. They knew they could appeal to Darius' pride and his desire for a unified kingdom.

i. "The suggested mode of compelling every subject in the former Babylonian domain to acknowledge the authority of Persia seemed a statesmanlike measure that would contribute to the unification of the Middle and Near East. The time limit of one month seemed reasonable." (Archer)

ii. "What pretence could they urge for so silly an ordinance? Probably to *flatter* the ambition of the king, they pretend to make him *a god* for *thirty* days; so that the whole empire should make prayer and supplication to him and pay him Divine honours! This was the bait; but their real object was to destroy Daniel." (Clarke)

iii. **All the governors of the kingdom, the administrators and satraps, the counselors and advisors, have consulted together**: Daniel's enemies also knew that people could be persuaded to do things they wouldn't normally do if they thought *everyone else* approved of that thing.

iv. Of course, they lied when they said **all the governors... have consulted together**. We know it was a lie because Daniel was one of the **governors** and he was not **consulted**.

e. **So that it cannot be changed, according to the law of the Medes and Persians**: It was an established principle in the Medo-Persian Empire that when a king formally signed and instituted a decree, it was so binding that not even the king himself could change it.

i. The decrees of a Persian king were unchangeable because he was thought to speak for the gods, who could never be wrong and thus never needed to change their minds.

f. **Therefore King Darius signed the written decree**: "Suppose the law of the land were proclaimed, 'No man shall pray during the remainder of this month, on pain of being cast into a den of lions,' - how many of you would pray? I think there would be rather a scanty number at the prayer-meeting. Not but what the attendance at prayer-meetings is scanty enough now! But if there were the penalty of being cast into a den of lions, I am afraid the prayer-meeting would be postponed for a month, owing to pressing business, and manifold engagements of one kind and another." (Spurgeon)

3. (10-15) Daniel's faithfulness to God causes him to be condemned to the lion's den.

Now when Daniel knew that the writing was signed, he went home. And in his upper room, with his windows open toward Jerusalem, he knelt down on his knees three times that day, and prayed and gave thanks before his God, as was his custom since early days. Then these men assembled and found Daniel praying and making supplication before his God. And they went before the king, and spoke concerning the king's decree: "Have you not signed a decree that every man who petitions any god or man within thirty days, except you, O king, shall be cast into the den of lions?" The king answered and said, "The thing *is* true, according to the law of the Medes and Persians, which does not alter." So they answered and said before the king, "That Daniel, who is one of the captives from Judah, does not show due regard for you, O king, or for the decree that you have signed, but makes his petition three times a day." And the king, when he heard *these* words, was greatly displeased with himself, and set *his* heart on Daniel to deliver him; and he labored till the going down of the sun to deliver him. Then these men approached the king, and said to the king, "Know, O king, that it is the law of the Medes and Persians that no decree or statute which the king establishes may be changed."

a. **When Daniel knew that the writing was signed**: Daniel was confronted with a test of loyalties. He was a loyal subject of his king, yet he knew that the King of Kings deserved a higher loyalty. Daniel refused to give to the government the measure of obedience that belonged to God alone.

i. Others perhaps considered it risky for Daniel to pray as was his custom. Daniel knew that the *safest* thing he could do was radically obey God.

ii. It isn't hard to see why people are men-pleasers; it *seems* as if people have the power to hire or fire us, to break our hearts, to slander us, to make our live generally miserable. The power to obey God and stand for Him comes from a settled understanding that God is really in control.

iii. "Unless you are prepared to be in the minority, and now and then to be called 'narrow,' 'fanatic,' and to be laughed at by men because you will not do what they do, but abstain and resist, then there is little chance of your ever making much of your Christian profession." (Maclaren)

b. **Prayed and gave thanks before his God, as was his custom since early days**: Daniel didn't let the decree change his actions one way or another. He didn't do more praying or less; he simply continued his excellent prayer life.

i. There was danger in both directions. It would have been compromise to do less or pride to do more. "This was not the act of a person courting martyrdom but the continuation of a faithful ministry in prayer which had characterized his long life." (Walvoord)

ii. What was Daniel's **custom** in prayer?

- He prayed **in his upper room** - this was private prayer, made with no intention to impress others.

- He prayed with **his windows open toward Jerusalem**, remembering the place of sacrifice even when there was no sacrifice.

- He prayed according to Scripture, because in 1 Kings 8 Solomon asked God to give special notice to the prayers of His people when they prayed towards Jerusalem and the temple: *And may You hear the supplication of Your servant and of Your people Israel, when they pray toward this place* (1 Kings 8:3).

- **He knelt down on his knees**, praying just as Jesus did, (Luke 22:41), as Stephen (Acts 7:60), as Peter (Acts 9:40), as Paul and other leaders in the church (Acts 20:36), and as Luke (Acts 21:5). "Kneeling is a begging posture and we must all come to God as beggars." (Heslop)

- He prayed **three times that day**, knowing that though a little prayer is good, much prayer is far better. We also remember that Daniel was one of three governors over an empire - yet still had time to pray. "That does not tell you how often he prayed, but how often he was in the posture of prayer. Doubtless he prayed 300 times a day if necessary - his heart was always having commerce with the skies; but thrice a day he prayed formally." (Spurgeon)

- He **prayed and gave thanks**, because great prayer is filled with thanksgiving. "Prayer and praise should always go up to heaven arm in arm, like twin angels walking up Jacob's ladder, or like kindred aspirations soaring up to the Most High." (Spurgeon)

c. **Found Daniel praying and making supplication before his God**: They found Daniel just as they knew they would - deep in prayer. For Daniel prayer was both communion with God and pleading for His will to be accomplished (**supplication**).

d. **Does not show due regard for you, O king**: This was not true. Daniel intended no disrespect for the king, only a higher respect for God.

e. **And the king, when he heard these words, was greatly displeased with himself**: There is a lot to like about King Darius, and one of the admirable things about him is that he was **displeased with himself**. Instead of blaming others, he knew that he was at fault. We can be sure that he wasn't happy with Daniel's enemies, but he knew that ultimately he was responsible.

> i. Like Darius, our foolish decisions often haunt us. Often all we can do is pray and ask God to mercifully and miraculously intervene when we make foolish decisions.

f. **He labored till the going down of the sun**: This means that he worked as long as he could. According to ancient eastern custom, the execution was carried out on the evening of the day that the accusation was made and found valid.

B. Daniel is preserved in the lion's den.

1. (16-18) Daniel's time in the lion's den.

So the king gave the command, and they brought Daniel and cast *him* into the den of lions. *But* the king spoke, saying to Daniel, "Your God, whom you serve continually, He will deliver you." Then a stone was brought and laid on the mouth of the den, and the king sealed it with his own signet ring and with the signets of his lords, that the purpose concerning Daniel might not be changed. Now the king went to his

palace and spent the night fasting; and no musicians were brought before him. Also his sleep went from him.

a. **Your God, whom you serve continually, He will deliver you**: Darius had faith, and it was faith born out of Daniel's trust in the Lord. The idea was, "I tried my best to save you Daniel, but I failed. Now it is up to your God."

b. **You serve continually**: This made Daniel's testimony. Many of us occasionally display godly character and wisdom before the world, but counter-act the good by then being bad. Daniel's testimony was made by *continual* service.

c. **The king sealed it**: This may have been to protect Daniel as much as to make sure someone didn't rescue Daniel. Darius knew that Daniel had powerful enemies who might kill him if the lions didn't.

d. **His sleep went from him**: Undoubtedly, Daniel had a better night's rest than Darius. We can be sure that Daniel prayed in the lions' den, because it was simply his habit to pray. He did not need to *start praying* on this remarkable occasion because the *habit of prayer* was well ingrained in his life.

i. "When our lives are centred in God, we can ever afford to leave circumstances to the compulsion of the One in Whom we trust. The occasional is always affected by the habitual." (Morgan)

ii. Perhaps Daniel prayed Psalm 22:21-22: *Save Me from the lion's mouth... I will declare Your name to My brethren; in the midst of the assembly I will praise You.*

iii. "In any case he must have had a glorious night. What with the lions, and with angels all night to keep him company, he was spending the night-watches in grander style than Darius." (Spurgeon)

2. (19-23) Daniel is found alive after the night in the lion's den.

Then the king arose very early in the morning and went in haste to the den of lions. And when he came to the den, he cried out with a lamenting voice to Daniel. The king spoke, saying to Daniel, "Daniel, servant of the living God, has your God, whom you serve continually, been able to deliver you from the lions?" Then Daniel said to the king, "O king, live forever! My God sent His angel and shut the lions' mouths, so that they have not hurt me, because I was found innocent before Him; and also, O king, I have done no wrong before you." Then the king was exceedingly glad for him, and commanded that they should take Daniel up out of the den. So Daniel was taken up out of the den, and no injury whatever was found on him, because he believed in his God.

a. **Very early in the morning**: Since he could not sleep, it was easy for Darius to rise **very early**. We imagine him waiting for the first glimmer of dawn so he could see how Daniel fared.

b. **Then Daniel said to the king**: When Darius heard Daniel's voice he knew that he had survived through the night. The lions would not or could not touch this servant of God.

c. **God sent His angel to shut the lions' mouth**: We don't know if Daniel *saw* an angel or not, but he certainly knew that **God sent His angel** to rescue him. Hebrews 1:14 says angels are *ministering spirits sent forth to minister for those who will inherit salvation*. God sent an angel to serve Daniel's need.

> i. "How the angel stopped the lions' mouths, whether by the brightness of his presence, or threatening them with his finger (Numbers 22:27, 33), or by making a rumble amongst them like that of an empty cart upon the stones, or by presenting unto them a light fire (which things lions are said to be terrified with), or by causing in them a satiety, or by working upon their fantasy, we need not inquire." (Trapp)

d. **I have done no wrong before you**: Daniel did break the king's law, but he did not go *against* the king or against the king's *best interests*. Daniel is an example of obedient disobedience.

e. **Because he believed in his God**: Daniel was preserved through *faith*. Though his cause was righteous and he was unjustly accused, those things alone did not protect him before the lions. Daniel needed a living, abiding faith in God, even in the most difficult circumstances.

> i. "Though they were savage and hunger-starved, yet Daniel was kept from the paws and jaws of these many fierce and fell lions by the power of God through faith." (Trapp)

> ii. There is an instructive order here. The power of God sent an angel to protect Daniel in response to a prayer of faith coming from a consistent, abiding walk.

> iii. Because of this faith, Daniel is recognized in Hebrews 11:33 as one who by faith *stopped the mouths of lions*.

3. (24) The fate of those who plotted against Daniel.

And the king gave the command, and they brought those men who had accused Daniel, and they cast *them* into the den of lions; them, their children, and their wives; and the lions overpowered them, and broke all their bones in pieces before they ever came to the bottom of the den.

a. **The king gave the command**: No one had to *ask* Darius to do this. He was ready and willing to bring justice to those who plotted against Daniel, and also to **their children, and their wives**.

i. This was obviously severe, but it was also according to ancient customs among the Persians. An ancient writer named Ammianus Marcellinus wrote of the Persians, "The laws among them are formidable... by which, on account of the guilt of one, all the kindred perish."

ii. Darius was not happy with these men. He probably would have cast these accusers to the lions even if Daniel *had* perished in the lion's den.

b. **The lions overpowered them... before they ever came to the bottom of the den**: This proved that it was genuinely angelic protection that saved Daniel. It proves there was no *natural* reason why the lions did not eat Daniel. Daniel's accusers perished in the same trap they set for Daniel.

i. This illustrates the work of the cross in reverse: the guilty were punished in the place of the innocent.

ii. This also illustrates a principle of spiritual warfare. God will cause our enemy to be impaled on the same snare set for us (Psalm 7:14-16).

4. (25-28) Darius decrees that all must honor the God of Daniel.

Then King Darius wrote:
To all peoples, nations, and languages that dwell in all the earth:
Peace be multiplied to you.
I make a decree that in every dominion of my kingdom *men must*
tremble and fear before the God of Daniel.
For He *is* **the living God,**
And steadfast forever;
His kingdom *is the one* **which shall not be destroyed,**
And His dominion *shall endure* **to the end.**
He delivers and rescues,
And He works signs and wonders
In heaven and on earth,
Who has delivered Daniel from the power of the lions.

So this Daniel prospered in the reign of Darius and in the reign of Cyrus the Persian.

a. **Then King Darius wrote**: The Book of Daniel follows a familiar pattern. God's people stand firm in their convictions, God honors and protects them, and the testimony of God's work makes the ungodly see and tell of the greatness of God.

- Daniel and his four friends stood firm and Nebuchadnezzar saw the fruit of it (Daniel 1:20).
- Daniel boldly and wisely interpreted Nebuchadnezzar's dream and the king honored Daniel and his God (Daniel 2:46-47).
- Shadrach, Meshach, and Abed-Nego stood firm and Nebuchadnezzar gave glory to God (Daniel 3:28-30).
- Daniel boldly told Nebuchadnezzar the truth and the king humbled himself and gave glory to God (Daniel 4:34-37).
- Daniel stood firm and boldly told Belshazzar the truth and the king honored Daniel (Daniel 5:29).

i. The point is plain: when we stand firm in godly convictions and honor God *even when it costs something*, others will see the testimony and be impressed.

b. **The God of Daniel**: In a small way, this helps us diagnose Darius' spiritual condition. It isn't enough to say, "**the God of Daniel**." Saving faith says, "the God of Darius."

c. **Daniel prospered in the reign of Darius and in the reign of Cyrus the Persian**: Some take this to mean that Darius *was* Cyrus the Persian. This is one of the three theories about the identity of Darius (mentioned at the beginning of this chapter).

d. **Daniel prospered**: This is the last link in a long chain set through this chapter. We can see Daniel progressing along this path:

- Plotted against.
- Praying.
- Praising.
- Persistently serving.
- Persecuted.
- Protected.
- Preserved.
- Preferred.
- Prospered.

e. **So Daniel prospered**: One of the greatest blessings to come from Daniel 6 is to see the story unfold and point to Jesus Christ. Consider this:

- A man without blame, faithful to God in all his ways, a man noted for prayer, was sent to his death because of the jealousy of those who wanted to prevent his exaltation.

- He was condemned to death by plotting of his enemies and the law of the land, and thrown into a stone room meant to be his tomb.

- A stone was rolled over the opening. But in all its power and ferocity, death couldn't touch him.

- On a morning the stone was rolled away, he came out victoriously; he glorified God, the pagans gave honor to God, and his enemies were judged.

- *That's a pretty good story* – the story of both Daniel 6 and Jesus the Messiah.

Daniel 7 - A Survey of Five World Empires

A. The four beasts.

1. (1) Introduction to the vision.

In the first year of Belshazzar king of Babylon, Daniel had a dream and visions of his head *while* on his bed. Then he wrote down the dream, telling the main facts.

a. **In the first year of Belshazzar**: This vision came to Daniel after the reign of Nebuchadnezzar, but before the Babylonian Empire was conquered by the Medo-Persian Empire.

i. Daniel chapters 1 through 6 describe the life and times of Daniel. Chapters 7 through 12 describe visions Daniel had. In order of events, the vision described in Daniel 7 took place during the time between Daniel chapters 4 and 5.

b. **Daniel had a dream and visions**: This first vision - one of four described between Daniel 7 through 12 - was the most comprehensive. The other three visions go into greater detail within the general framework of this first vision.

c. **Telling the main facts**: Daniel *could have* given us more detail but the Holy Spirit only wanted him to write the **main facts**. We may wish that Daniel went into greater detail, but he didn't.

2. (2-3) Four beasts and where they come from.

Daniel spoke, saying, "I saw in my vision by night, and behold, the four winds of heaven were stirring up the Great Sea. And four great beasts came up from the sea, each different from the other."

a. **Stirring up the Great Sea**: This was almost certainly the Mediterranean Sea. Each one of the empires mentioned in this vision had a geographical connection to the Mediterranean Sea.

i. **Stirring up** has the idea of chaos and tumult. "To the Hebrews the sea was both dangerous and mysterious, a restless element but not beyond the Lord's power to tame." (Baldwin)

ii. The sea is sometimes used as a picture of Gentile nations (Psalm 74:13, Psalm 89:9, Isaiah 57:20).

b. **The four winds of heaven**: Some see these **winds** as a description of the sovereign power of God striving with men (as in Psalm 35:5, Psalm 48:7, Psalm 107:25 Isaiah 27:8 and Isaiah 41:16). Others (such as Strauss) suggest the four winds were satanic forces, as mentioned in Revelation 7:1.

c. **And four great beasts came up from the sea**: Four large, ferocious animals emerged from the Great Sea, each one distinct from the other.

3. (4-6) A description of the first three beasts.

The first *was* like a lion, and had eagle's wings. I watched till its wings were plucked off; and it was lifted up from the earth and made to stand on two feet like a man, and a man's heart was given to it. And suddenly another beast, a second, like a bear. It was raised up on one side, and *had* three ribs in its mouth between its teeth. And they said thus to it: "Arise, devour much flesh!" After this I looked, and there was another, like a leopard, which had on its back four wings of a bird. The beast also had four heads, and dominion was given to it.

a. **The first was like a lion**: The first beast was more majestic than any of the following beasts (lions and eagles are "kings" of their realms). But this majestic beast was humbled (**wings were plucked off**) and made human (**a man's heart was given to it**).

i. A little later (Daniel 7:17) Daniel tells us that these four beasts are four kingdoms ruling over the earth. The first kingdom is the Babylonian Empire, represented by a **lion** and an **eagle**. This fits in well with the majesty and authority of Nebuchadnezzar in his reign over the empire of Babylon.

ii. Jeremiah used both the lion and the eagle as pictures of Nebuchadnezzar (Jeremiah 49:19-22), and Babylon's winged lions can be seen at the British Museum today.

b. **A second, like a bear**: The second beast didn't have the majestic bearing of either the lion or the eagle. A **bear** is slower, stronger, and more crushing than a lion - and this bear had a voracious appetite for conquest (**Arise, devour much flesh!**).

i. The **bear** represented the Medo-Persian Empire, succeeding the Babylonian Empire. In this partnership between the Medes and the

Persians, the Persians dominated the relationship. Most think the **three ribs** represent their three great military conquests: Babylon, Egypt and Lydia.

ii. The slow, crushing armies of the Medo-Persian Empire were well known. They simply overwhelmed their opponents with superior size and strength. "The Medes and Persians are compared to a *bear* on account of their *cruelty* and *thirst after blood*, a bear being a most voracious and cruel animal." (Clarke)

iii. **Arise, devour much flesh**: "The command to arise and devour much flesh indicates the extreme cruelties often practiced by the Persians, and the wide extent of their conquests." (Ironside)

iv. Liberal commentators have a vested interest in identifying the bear with *only* the Median state, and not the combined Medo-Persian Empire. They assign the third beast to the Persian Empire, and the fourth to Alexander's Greek Empire, so as to remove (even for a second century author) any element of predictive prophecy. Their analysis doesn't fit. There are many good reasons why the second kingdom could not be exclusively the Median kingdom.

- The Median kingdom did not follow the Babylonian in historical sequence, but was contemporary with it, even rising to strength *before* the Neo-Babylonian period.

- The Median kingdom never had a world position ranking with the Persian, Grecian or Babylonian Empires.

- The motivation for the interpretation is solely to remove any reference to Rome - and to divinely predictive prophecy.

c. **Another, like a leopard**: The **leopard** was known for its sudden, unexpected attacks. This one was especially swift (with **four wings**), and clever (having **four heads**).

i. Each animal is mighty, but dominates its prey in a different way. "The lion devours, the bear crushes, and the leopard springs upon its prey." (Strauss)

ii. The **leopard** represented the Greek Empire. Alexander the Great quickly conquered the civilized world by age 28. "Nothing in the history of the world, was equal to the conquests of Alexander, who ran through all the countries from Illycrium and the Adriatic Sea to the Indian Ocean and the River Ganges; and in *twelve* years subdued part of Europe, and all Asia." (Clarke)

iii. After his death his empire was divided into four parts (**four heads**). Specifically, the four heads were Casander, Lysimachus, Seleucus, and Ptolemy, who inherited Alexander's domain after his death.

iv. The Babylonian Empire dominated in Daniel's day. One might have guessed - especially in the reign of Belshazzar - that the next empire would be the Medo-Persian Empire. But how could Daniel know that the next world empire would be like a leopard in its rise and prominence, and that it would be divided into four parts? This shows a plain principle: God knows the future, and reveals certain details of the future through His prophets. It shows that God lives outside our time domain and can see the future as well as the past. He sees the whole parade of human history, not just the part passing in front of a single spectator. The proof of fulfilled prophecy is exceptionally persuasive; no wonder Peter says: *We have the prophetic word confirmed, which you do well to heed as a light that shines in a dark place, until the day dawns and the morning star rises in your hearts* (2 Peter 1:19).

4. (7-8) The fourth beast: a dreadful, horned beast, with one conspicuous horn.

After this I saw in the night visions, and behold, a fourth beast, dreadful and terrible, exceedingly strong. It had huge iron teeth; it was devouring, breaking in pieces, and trampling the residue with its feet. It *was* different from all the beasts that *were* before it, and it had ten horns. I was considering the horns, and there was another horn, a little one, coming up among them, before whom three of the first horns were plucked out by the roots. And there, in this horn, *were* eyes like the eyes of a man, and a mouth speaking pompous words.

a. **A fourth beast, dreadful and terrible**: The fourth beast was indescribable, and uniquely horrific in its power and conquest.

b. **Different... it had ten horns**: In the ancient world **horns** expressed the power and fearsomeness of an animal. This fourth beast was so strong it had **ten horns**.

i. Different people picture this different ways. Some suggest that the ten horns were actually two five-pointed antlers, rather than ten separate horns.

ii. In historical fulfillment, the fourth beast represents the Roman Empire, which was the largest, strongest, most unified and enduring of them all.

iii. "There is an unmistakable correspondence between these horns and the ten toes of the dream image (ch. 2), and the mention of iron in the teeth suggests the legs and toes of iron in that image." (Archer)

c. **Another horn, a little one... a mouth speaking pompous words**: Among the ten horns, three are replaced by one horn that was conspicuous for its dominance (**before whom three of the first horns were plucked out by the roots**), intelligence (**eyes like the eyes of a man**), and its boastful talk (**speaking pompous words**).

5. (9-10) The *Ancient of Days* and the scene surrounding his throne.

I watched till thrones were put in place,
And the Ancient of Days was seated;
His garment *was* **white as snow,**
And the hair of His head *was* **like pure wool.**
His throne *was* **a fiery flame,**
Its wheels a burning fire;
A fiery stream issued
And came forth from before Him.
A thousand thousands ministered to Him;
Ten thousand times ten thousand stood before Him.
The court was seated,
And the books were opened.

a. **I watched till thrones were put in place**: The King James Version poorly translates this as *thrones were cast down*. The New King James Version corrected this and indicates that the **thrones** were established.

i. When the Apostle John saw heaven, he also saw **thrones**, but he also saw those who sat on those thrones - the 24 elders described in Revelation 4:4. Daniel made no mention of these elders, perhaps because the 24 elders represent the church, and the church was an unrevealed mystery to Old Testament saints (Ephesians 3:1-7).

b. **And the Ancient of Days was seated**: The **Ancient of Days** is obviously God, but there is debate as to if He is specifically God the Father or God the Son. Most believe it is God the Father, and the white garments and white hair stress the eternal character of God the Father.

i. Daniel 7:13 seems to make a distinction between the **Ancient of Days** and the *Son of Man*, and this supports the idea that the **Ancient of Days** is God the Father, not God the Son.

ii. "We ought not to imagine God in his essence to be like any appearance to his own Prophet and other holy fathers, but he put on various appearances, according to man's comprehension, to whom he wished to give some signs of his presence." (Calvin)

c. **His throne was a fiery flame**: This was a brilliant manifestation of God's splendor and the fierce heat of His judgment. There seems to be something lava-like in the stream of fire pouring from the throne; it was like a river of vast destructive power.

i. Isaiah 66:15-15 describes the judgment of God in terms of fire: *For behold, the* LORD *will come with fire and with His chariots, like a whirlwind, to render His anger with fury, and His rebuke with flames of fire. For by fire and by His sword the* LORD *will judge all flesh; and the slain of the* LORD *shall be many.*

d. **Its wheels a burning fire**: Many commentators say that in the ancient eastern world royal thrones were often on wheels. Yet it is just as likely that they represent the endless activity of God.

e. **A thousand thousands ministered to Him**: This describes the innumerable company of angels surrounding the throne of God.

f. **Ten thousand times ten thousand stood before Him**: This describes humanity standing before God in judgment.

g. **Court was seated, and the books were opened**: The Bible describes several books before God, and any of these or combination of these could be meant.

- The book of the living (Psalm 69:28).
- The book of remembrance (Malachi 3:16).
- The Book of Life (Philippians 4:3, Revelation 3:5; 13:8; 17:8; 20:12, 15; 21:27 and 22:19).

6. (11-14) The conspicuous horn is conquered by the Son of Man.

I watched then because of the sound of the pompous words which the horn was speaking; I watched till the beast was slain, and its body destroyed and given to the burning flame. As for the rest of the beasts, they had their dominion taken away, yet their lives were prolonged for a season and a time.

I was watching in the night visions,
And behold, *one* **like the Son of Man,**
Coming with the clouds of heaven!
He came to the Ancient of Days,
And they brought Him near before Him.
Then to Him was given dominion and glory and a kingdom,
That all peoples, nations, and languages should serve Him.
His dominion *is* **an everlasting dominion,**
Which shall not pass away,
And His kingdom *the one*
Which shall not be destroyed.

a. **They had their dominion taken away**: This great passage describes the transition from *human* dominion on earth to *divine* dominion. This happens as **the Son of Man** comes and exercises dominion over the earth. The **Son of Man** succeeds the reign of the fourth beast.

b. **The sound of the pompous words which the horn was speaking**: Here the "little horn" of the fourth beast again speaks **pompous words**. The final human dictator we commonly call the Antichrist will be characterized by his boastful, blasphemous speech (Revelation 13:5-6).

i. Because of the distinction between the fourth beast and the horn, some conjecture that the beast of Revelation 13 is not the Antichrist but his government or administration. If this is so, it is a small distinction. To a large extent, a man does represent and personify an entire government or system. When we think of Germany in the 1930s and 1940s, the figures of Hitler as an individual and Nazi Germany as a state are virtually the same.

c. **I watched till the beast was slain... the rest of the beasts, they had their dominion taken away**: The fourth beast is destroyed and the others may continue, but without **dominion** of their own. When Jesus sets up His kingdom, the empire of the Antichrist will be completely crushed, yet some nations will continue into the Millennium.

d. **One like the Son of Man, coming with the clouds of heaven**: The title **Son of Man** was a favorite self-designation of Jesus, used more than 80 times in the four Gospels. He receives all dominion previously held by the beasts and His reign will be permanent.

e. **His dominion is an everlasting dominion, which shall not pass away**: The reign of Jesus does not last 1,000 years - it is permanent. However, Jesus will rule over this earth before it is remade, with Satan bound for 1,000 years.

B. Interpretation of the dream.

1. (15-16) Daniel's reaction to the vision and request for understanding.

I, Daniel, was grieved in my spirit within *my* body, and the visions of my head troubled me. I came near to one of those who stood by, and asked him the truth of all this. So he told me and made known to me the interpretation of these things:

a. **Was grieved in my spirit**: Daniel saw all this, and in more detail than he describes for us. He did not really understand all that he saw, and was troubled because of his lack of understanding.

b. **Grieved in my spirit within my body**: This shows that our **spirit** indeed dwells **within** the **body**. It is true that the spirit is more important than the body (1 Timothy 4:8), but the state of the body generally has an effect on the state of the spirit.

i. Clarke says that the phrase **my spirit within my body** has the sense of "within its sheath or scabbard." From this, Clarke says: "Which I think proves, 1. That the human *spirit* is different from the *body*. 2. That it has a proper subsistence independently of the body, which is only its *sheath* for a certain time. 3. That the spirit may exist independently of the body, as the *sword* does independently of its *sheath*."

2. (17-18) Summary of the vision: four kings are conquered by God, and their kingdoms are given to the people of God.

Those great beasts, which are four, *are* four kings *which* arise out of the earth. "But the saints of the Most High shall receive the kingdom, and possess the kingdom forever, even forever and ever."

a. **Those great beasts, which are four, are four kings which arise out of the earth**: The divine interpretation of the dream shows that this vision covers the same material as Nebuchadnezzar's vision in Daniel 2, which also described the rise of four empires, which are succeeded by the kingdom of God.

i. Yet Daniel's vision was different, seeing the kingdoms from God's perspective, not man's. Nebuchadnezzar saw the present and future world empires in the form of a stately and noble statue of a man. Here God showed how He regarded them: as ferocious and wild animals who devour and conquer without conscience.

ii. When man writes his own history, there is often much self-congratulation and man seems to be on the verge of paradise. When God writes human history, a different vision is presented.

iii. Jesus is the Lion of the Tribe of Judah (Revelation 5:5). Yet He primarily represents Himself not as a ferocious animal but as a lamb (Revelation 5:5-6 and 5:8-10).

b. **The saints of the Most High shall receive the kingdom**: When the day of the fourth beast is over, then God's people **receive the kingdom**. Yet we know the Roman Empire is long gone - and it doesn't seem that the saints have received the kingdom.

i. This is what prompts many to look for either a spiritualized interpretation fulfilled in history, or some kind of restoration of the Roman Empire in the last days, one that will literally fulfill the prophecy of the ten horns and the little horn as well.

ii. **Shall receive the kingdom**: The saints **receive the kingdom**. God gives them the kingdom at the return of Jesus. They do not gain dominion over all these earthly kingdoms before the return of Jesus.

3. (19-22) Daniel's specific request to know about the conspicuous horn.

Then I wished to know the truth about the fourth beast, which was different from all the others, exceedingly dreadful, *with* its teeth of iron and its nails of bronze, *which* devoured, broke in pieces, and trampled the residue with its feet; and the ten horns that *were* on its head, and the other *horn* which came up, before which three fell, namely, that horn which had eyes and a mouth which spoke pompous words, whose appearance *was* greater than his fellows. I was watching; and the same horn was making war against the saints, and prevailing against them, until the Ancient of Days came, and a judgment was made *in favor* of the saints of the Most High, and the time came for the saints to possess the kingdom.

a. **I wished to know the truth about the fourth beast**: There was much interest in all these four beasts, but Daniel was *especially* interested in the fourth, most terrible beast - and especially about its conspicuous **horn**.

b. **Exceedingly dreadful, with its teeth of iron and its nails of bronze**: The fourth beast interested Daniel because of its great destructive power, because of the conspicuous horn, and because of its fight against God's people (**the same horn was making war against the saints**).

i. If this horn represents the Antichrist, and he fights **against the saints**, it does not necessarily mean that the church will be on earth as a target of the Antichrist during the tribulation. We can say, "Not necessarily," because **saints** can indicate the church *or* a Jewish remnant in the tribulation (Revelation 12:17; 13:7).

4. (23-27) The meaning of the conspicuous horn and its defeat.

"Thus he said:
'The fourth beast shall be
A fourth kingdom on earth,
Which shall be different from all *other* kingdoms,
And shall devour the whole earth,
Trample it and break it in pieces.
The ten horns *are* ten kings
***Who* shall arise from this kingdom.**
And another shall rise after them;
He shall be different from the first *ones*,
And shall subdue three kings.

He shall speak *pompous* words against the Most High,
Shall persecute the saints of the Most High,
And shall intend to change times and law.
Then *the saints* shall be given into his hand
For a time and times and half a time.
'But the court shall be seated,
And they shall take away his dominion,
To consume and destroy *it* forever.
Then the kingdom and dominion,
And the greatness of the kingdoms under the whole heaven,
Shall be given to the people, the saints of the Most High.
His kingdom *is* an everlasting kingdom,
And all dominions shall serve and obey Him.'

a. **The fourth beast shall be a fourth kingdom on earth**: This initial description of the **fourth beast** fits well with the Roman Empire of ancient history. It did **devour the whole** civilized **earth**, and dominate it completely for about a thousand years.

b. **The ten horns are ten kings who shall arise from this kingdom**: These **ten kings** *do not* have a literal fulfillment in the Roman Empire of history. If they are literal, they are still in the future. The only way to say this has been fulfilled is to spiritualize this prophecy and take away its plain sense.

i. Many, like John Calvin, merely spiritualize this. He insisted that what happened in this chapter was fulfilled in history up unto the time of Jesus' first advent, and supposed that the ten horns merely represent a multiplicity of kings under the Roman emperor, and believed that the conspicuous horn was Julius Caesar and the other Caesars who succeeded him. And for Calvin, *the books were opened* (verse 10) referred to the preaching of the gospel.

ii. But if there are ten toes (Daniel 2) and ten horns (Daniel 7 and Revelation 13 and 17) associated with the rule of this final world ruler, there is no good reason to spiritualize what God has said in at least four different places.

iii. The same spiritualizing problems apply if one believes that this is fulfilled in the early church and the passing of the Roman Empire (unlike Calvin who saw fulfillment before the first advent of Jesus).

iv. The conspicuous horn must be the Antichrist, arising out of some group of ten nations that is in some way part of a restored Roman Empire.

c. **He shall speak pompous words against the Most High**: The little horn spoke pompous, blasphemous words, perhaps like the Fascist Creed of Italy (cited in Talbot):

> i. "I believe in Rome Eternal, the Mother of my fatherland; and in Italy, her first born; who was born of her virgin womb by the grace of God; who suffered under the barbarian invader, was crucified, slain, and buried; who descended into the sepulcher, and rose from the dead in the nineteenth century; who ascended to heaven in her glory in 1918 and 1922 [by the march on Rome]; who is seated at the right hand of Mother Rome; who will come thence to judge the quick and the dead; I believe in the genius of Mussolini; in our Holy Father, Fascism, and in the communion of its martyrs; in the conversion of the Italians; and in the resurrection of the Empire! Amen."

d. **Shall persecute the saints of the Most High**: This speaks of a cruel and systematic pressure, coming from the word "to wear away" or "to wear out," as friction wears clothes or shoes.

> i. "To wear out the saints means to harass them continually so that life becomes a wretched existence." (Wood)

> ii. "Such continual and protracted pressure far more effectively breaks the human spirit than the single moment of crisis that calls for a heroic decision. It is easier to die for the Lord than to live for him under constant harassment and strain." (Archer)

> iii. "The Bible predicts no peace-loving world ruler for the last days. We can expect nothing more than greedy commercialism and political imperialism under the most beastly and barbaric type of warfare." (Strauss)

e. **Shall intend to change times and law**: This little horn will **intend** to change times and law perhaps as at the French Revolution, where radicals wanted to institute a ten-day work week, and declared 1792 (the year of the Revolution) as year 1.

> i. Seventh-Day Adventists have historically taught that it was the Papacy which "changed the times and law" by moving the Lord's day from Saturday to Sunday. Some traditional Seventh-Day Adventists therefore regard Sunday worship as the sign of the Antichrist.

f. **Then the saints shall be given into his hand for a time and times and half a time**: The power of the little horn over the **saints** is limited. It will last for three-and-one-half years (**time and times and half a time**). This phrase is used in Revelation (11:2-3, 12:6 and 13:5) to refer to half of the last seven-year period of man's rule on this earth (the seventieth week of Daniel).

g. They shall take away his dominion, to consume and destroy it forever: In the day of persecution by this blasphemous ruler, the Messiah will establish His kingdom for His people.

i. Because the kingdom of Jesus immediately succeeds this fourth kingdom, no event in the past answers this prediction in the smallest degree. Certainly, the church did not cause a sudden and catastrophic fall of the Roman Empire. "It is questionable whether the Roman Empire had any serious opposition from the Christian church or that the growing power of the church contributed in a major way to its downfall." (Walvoord)

ii. There are three options in interpreting the kingdom's establishment here:

- There is no fulfillment; Daniel is in error.
- The fulfillment is symbolic in church history.
- The fulfillment is literal, and yet future.

h. Then the kingdom and dominion, and the greatness of the kingdoms under the whole heaven, shall be given to the people, the saints of the Most High: This must describe the millennial earth, not our current age or heaven. The **kingdom and dominion** of the earth certainly does not belong to the righteous now. If this describes the eternal state, then what are the **dominions** that **shall serve and obey Him**? It therefore must describe the millennial earth.

i. We again notice that the **kingdom and dominion... shall be given to the** saints. It is something received, not achieved. The church does not convert the world to Jesus' kingdom and give the kingdom to Jesus; He gives it to them.

5. (28) Daniel's troubled reaction to the vision and its interpretation.

"This *is* the end of the account. As for me, Daniel, my thoughts greatly troubled me, and my countenance changed; but I kept the matter in my heart."

a. **My thoughts greatly troubled me**: Many things might trouble Daniel at this vision - such as the ferocity of the attack to come against his people from the conspicuous horn.

b. **And my countenance changed**: Daniel was convinced that the prophecy was true, and that it was the word of God. He was so convinced of its truth that his **countenance changed** and he considered what would happen.

Daniel 8 - Antiochus and Antichrist

In the ancient manuscripts, the Book of Daniel here resumes using the Hebrew language. The section from Daniel 2:4 to 7:28 was written in Aramaic.

A. The vision recounted.

1. (1-2) Introduction to the vision.

In the third year of the reign of King Belshazzar a vision appeared *to* me; to me, Daniel; after the one that appeared to me the first time. I saw in the vision, and it so happened while I was looking, that I *was* in Shushan, the citadel, which *is* in the province of Elam; and I saw in the vision that I was by the River Ulai.

a. **The third year of the reign of King Belshazzar**: This vision happened while Babylon was securely in power. Though the vision will deal with the emergence and destiny of the Greek Empire, the Greek Empire was not much of anything at the time the prophecy came to Daniel.

b. **I was in Shushan, the citadel**: Daniel was in **Shushan** on business for the king (Daniel 8:27).

2. (3-4) A mighty ram pushing in different directions.

Then I lifted my eyes and saw, and there, standing beside the river, was a ram which had two horns, and the two horns *were* high; but one *was* higher than the other, and the higher *one* came up last. I saw the ram pushing westward, northward, and southward, so that no animal could withstand him; nor *was there any* that could deliver from his hand, but he did according to his will and became great.

a. **A ram which had two horns**: In this same chapter (Daniel 8:20) this **ram** was clearly identified as representing the Medo-Persian Empire, which succeeded the Babylonian Empire.

i. It wasn't a stretch to use a **ram** to represent the Medo-Persian Empire. "Ammianus Marcellinus, a fourth century historian, states that the Persian ruler bore the head of a ram as he stood at the head of his army." (Wood) "The ram was the national emblem of Persia, a ram being stamped on Persian coins as well as on the headdress of Persian emperors." (Strauss)

b. **The two horns were high; but one was higher than the other**: The ram was noted for the proportion of its two horns - **one was higher than the other**. This was an accurate prediction of the partnership between the Medes and the Persians, because the Persians were larger and stronger in the partnership. They also emerged *after* the Medes (**the higher one came up last**).

c. **Pushing westward, northward, and southward**: The Medo-Persian Empire exerted its power to the north, south, and west. It took territory but made no major conquests towards the east.

> i. "The principle theatre of their wars, says *Calmet*, was against the SCYTHIANS, *northward*; against the GREEKS, *westward*; and against the EGYPTIANS, *southward*." (Clarke)

3. (5-8) A male goat challenges and conquers the ram.

And as I was considering, suddenly a male goat came from the west, across the surface of the whole earth, without touching the ground; and the goat *had* a notable horn between his eyes. Then he came to the ram that had two horns, which I had seen standing beside the river, and ran at him with furious power. And I saw him confronting the ram; he was moved with rage against him, attacked the ram, and broke his two horns. There was no power in the ram to withstand him, but he cast him down to the ground and trampled him; and there was no one that could deliver the ram from his hand. Therefore the male goat grew very great; but when he became strong, the large horn was broken, and in place of it four notable ones came up toward the four winds of heaven.

a. **A male goat came from the west**: In this same chapter (Daniel 8:21-22) this **male goat** was clearly identified with Greece and its horns are identified with the rulers of the Greek Empire.

> i. From ancient history we know this wasn't a strange symbol. The goat was a common representation of the Greek Empire. "*Newton* very properly observes that, *two hundred* years before the time of Daniel, they were called, the *goats' people*." (Clarke)

b. **Across the surface of the whole earth, without touching the ground**: This prophetic description of the male goat was proved to be accurate regarding the Greek Empire.

- The Greek Empire rose **from the west** of previous empires.

- The Greek Empire rose with great speed (**suddenly... without touching the ground**).
- The Greek Empire had a notable ruler, Alexander the Great (**a notable horn**).
- The Greek Empire had a famous war with the Medo-Persian Empire (**I saw him confronting the ram**).
- The Greek Empire and the Medo-Persian Empire greatly hated each other (**with furious power... moved with rage**). Some of the greatest, fiercest battles of ancient history were fought between the Greeks and the Persians.
- The Greek Empire conquered the Medo-Persian Empire (**no one that could deliver the ram from his hand**).
- The reign of the notable leader of the Greek Empire was suddenly cut short (**the large horn was broken**).
- After the end of Alexander the Great's reign, the Greek Empire was divided among four rulers (**in place of it four notable ones came up**).
- The four rulers of the Greek Empire after Alexander ruled their own dominions, not the entire empire together (**came up toward the four winds of heaven**).

  i. Alexander did not divide the empire among his four generals himself. His four leading generals divided it among themselves by force after his death. The four generals were:

    - Cassander, ruling over Greece and its region.
    - Lysimachus, ruling over Asia Minor.
    - Seleucus, ruling over Syria and Israel's land.
    - Ptolemy, ruling over Egypt.

c. **The male goat grew very great**: The greatness of Alexander's Empire was not only in its vast dominion but also in its cultural power. Alexander the Great was determined to spread Greek civilization, culture, and language across every land he conquered.

  i. As God guided history, He used Alexander's passion to spread Greek culture to prepare the world for the Gospel of Jesus Christ. Because of Alexander's influence, *koine* (common) Greek became the common language of the civilized world - and the language of the New Testament.

4. (9-12) The strong horn that arises from the four horns of the male goat.

And out of one of them came a little horn which grew exceedingly great toward the south, toward the east, and toward the Glorious *Land*. And it grew up to the host of heaven; and it cast down *some* of the host and *some* of the stars to the ground, and trampled them. He even exalted *himself* as high as the Prince of the host; and by him the daily *sacrifices* were taken away, and the place of His sanctuary was cast down. Because of transgression, an army was given over *to the horn* to oppose the daily *sacrifices;* and he cast truth down to the ground. He did *all this* and prospered.

a. **A little horn which grew exceeding great**: This was fulfilled in one of the four successors to Alexander the Great. Since the dominion of this horn was extended **toward the south, toward the east, and toward the Glorious Land**, we can identify the historical fulfillment of this **little horn** in Antiochus IV Epiphanes who ruled over Syria and Israel's land under the Seleucid dynasty.

i. Israel's land was contested between the dynasties of Seleucid and Ptolemy, but the Seleucids gained power over the region in the days of Antiochus III (198 b.c.).

ii. Antiochus IV gained the throne of his father (Antiochus III) by murdering his brother, the former king Seleucus Philopator. The son of Philopator was the rightful heir to the throne, but Antiochus IV had him held hostage in Rome. Antiochus IV legitimized his rule mainly through flattery and bribery.

iii. Antiochus IV assumed the title *Epiphanes* meaning, "illustrious" and alluding to deity. The ancient Jews twisted his name into "*Epimanes*" meaning, "madman."

b. **The Glorious Land**: In the Hebrew, the same term was used for the land of Israel in Ezekiel 20:6 (*the glory of all lands*), Ezekiel 25:9 (*the glory of the country*), and in Daniel 11:16 and 11:41. Similar wording is used in Psalm 48:2.

i. We can rightly see the **Glorious Land** as the center of the world:

- It is the *nerve center* of civilization since the days of Abraham.

- It is the *truth center* from which flowed God's revelation to man.

- It is the *storm center* of warring nations since the days of Joshua.

- It will be the *peace center* of the earth during the millennial reign of Jesus.

- It will be the *home center* for the Jewish people forever more.

c. **He even exalted himself as high as the Prince of the host**: Antiochus Epiphanes was an accurate and dramatic fulfillment of this prophecy in history - so much so that critics insist that the Book of Daniel *must* have been written *after* his time.

i. Antiochus Epiphanes exerted his dominion **toward the south, toward the east, and toward the** land of Israel.

ii. Antiochus Epiphanes murdered other rulers and persecuted the people of Israel (**cast down some of the host and some of the stars to the ground, and trampled them**).

iii. Antiochus Epiphanes blasphemed God and commanded idolatrous worship directed towards himself (**exalted himself as high as the Prince of the host**).

iv. Antiochus Epiphanes put a stop to temple sacrifices in Jerusalem (**by him the daily sacrifices were taken away**).

v. Antiochus Epiphanes desecrated the temple (**the place of His sanctuary was cast down**).

vi. Antiochus Epiphanes opposed God and seemed to prosper (**he cast truth down to the ground. He did all this and prospered**).

d. **It cast down some of the host and some of the stars to the ground**: The **host** and **stars** are symbols used in the Old Testament for angels, kings and leaders, or the people of God at large. This prediction was fulfilled in Antiochus Epiphanes and his attacks against rulers and against God's people in general.

i. The terms *stars of heaven* (Genesis 12:3 and 15:5) and the *hosts of the LORD* (Exodus 12:41) are at times used of God's people in general.

ii. "Undoubtedly it is the design here to describe the pride and ambition of [the 'little horn'], and to show that he did not think anything too exalted for his aspiration." (Barnes)

e. **And trampled them**: Antiochus was an infamous persecutor of the Jewish people. He wanted them to submit to Greek culture and customs and was more than willing to use murder and violence to compel them.

i. Antiochus's suppression of the Jews came to a head in December of 168 B.C. when he returned in defeat from Alexandria. He ordered his generals to seize Jerusalem on a Sabbath. There he set up an idol of Zeus and desecrated the altar by an offering of swine and sprinkling the pig's juices in the sanctuary. Sacrifice stopped because the temple was desecrated.

ii. 1 Maccabees 1:29-32 and 1:52-61 describe how Antiochus persecuted the Jews. 1 Maccabees 1:41-50 describes his blasphemies (see Appendix A, page 139). By some estimates he was responsible for the murder of more than 100,000 Jews.

f. **Because of transgression, an army was given over to the horn to oppose the daily sacrifices**: This was fulfilled in the terrors of Antiochus Epiphanes. The Jews, especially their leaders, invited God's judgment upon them through Antiochus because of their sin.

i. The first attack of Antiochus against the Jews of this time was to settle a rivalry for the office of high priest. A pious high priest, Onias III, was removed from office and was replaced with his brother Jason because Jason bribed Antiochus. Then in 172 B.C. another brother (Menelaus) gave Antiochus an even bigger bribe and replaced Jason. A year later Menelaus started selling many of the temple's gold utensils to raise money to pay off the bribe. Onias III rebuked him, and Menelaus had him murdered. Meanwhile, Jason gathered armies and fought against Menelaus to regain the office of High Priest. Antiochus Epiphanes came in to Jerusalem in 171 B.C. to defend the man who paid him a bigger bribe to be the High Priest.

ii. "This was the reason why God set over them such a breathing devil, as was Antiochus, for a punishment of their open impiety and formal apostasy." (Trapp)

5. (13-14) The duration of the sanctuary's desecration: 2,300 days.

Then I heard a holy one speaking; and *another* holy one said to that certain *one* who was speaking, "How long *will* the vision *be, concerning* the daily *sacrifices* and the transgression of desolation, the giving of both the sanctuary and the host to be trampled under foot?" And he said to me, "For two thousand three hundred days; then the sanctuary shall be cleansed."

a. **Then I heard a holy one speaking**: Many think this nameless **holy one** is an Old Testament appearance of Jesus. This is possible, but there is not enough information to be certain.

b. **How long will the vision be?** Daniel didn't ask this question; he heard the holy ones speaking together and one of them asked the question. They wanted to know how long the **sacrifices** would be suspended and how long the **sanctuary** would be desecrated.

c. **For two thousand three hundred days**: Literally, Daniel heard a holy one say "**two thousand three hundred** *mornings and evenings*." Bible students debate if this means 2,300 days or 1,150 days. 2,300 days is almost seven years.

i. Either understanding is possible, but it is more likely that this means 2,300 days. The date when the temple was cleansed is well established as December 25, 165 B.C. If we count back 2,300 days from then, we come to the year when Antiochus Epiphanes began his persecution in earnest (171 B.C.).

ii. However, if we take it to mean 1,150 days it can refer to the time the temple was actually desecrated. Philip Newell makes this case: "For a duration of time during which 2300 daily sacrifices would ordinarily have been offered, one at evening and one in the morning, as specified in Exodus 29:38-43. Since there are two of these daily, the actual time period involved is 1150 days, or slightly over three years. This, in fact, was the time of the Maccabean tribulation, 168-165 B.C., at the end of which the sanctuary was 'cleansed' by Judas Maccabeus in his restoration of the evening and morning sacrifices (2 Maccabees 10:1-5)."

iii. This passage has been a favorite springboard for elaborate and fanciful prophetic interpretations. A popular and tragic interpretation of this passage took one year for every day, and William Miller used 2,300 "year-days" to calculate that Jesus would return in 1844 (2,300 years after Cyrus issued the decree to rebuild the temple). His movement ended up giving birth to the Seventh-Day Adventists, the Jehovah's Witnesses, and several other movements.

iv. We can know that Miller and other "year-day" theories are wrong because this passage was fulfilled before the time of Jesus. Jesus recognized that the temple was properly **cleansed** and rededicated when He attended the Feast of Dedication, commemorating the cleansing and rededication of the temple after the desecration brought by Antiochus Epiphanes (John 10:22).

v. Adam Clarke's comments show what a hold the year-date approach had to many of his time: "Though literally it be *two thousand three hundred evenings and mornings*, yet I think the *prophetic day* should be understood here, as in other parts of this prophet, and must signify so many *years*. If we date these years from the vision of the he-goat, (Alexander's invading Asia), this was A.M. 3670, B.C. 334; and *two thousand three hundred years* from that time will reach to A.D. 1966, or *one hundred and forty-one* years from the present A.D. 1825." There is no foundation for Clarke's approach, and it has led many others off into serious error.

d. **Then the sanctuary shall be cleansed**: This amazingly specific prophecy was written some 350 years before the time of Antiochus Epiphanes. Great prophetic fulfillment like this demonstrates that God not only *knows* the future, He also *guides* the future.

B. The vision is interpreted.

1. (15-19) Gabriel appears to Daniel.

Then it happened, when I, Daniel, had seen the vision and was seeking the meaning, that suddenly there stood before me one having the appearance of a man. And I heard a man's voice between *the banks of the Ulai*, who called, and said, "Gabriel, make this *man* understand the vision." So he came near where I stood, and when he came I was afraid and fell on my face; but he said to me, "Understand, son of man, that the vision *refers* to the time of the end." Now, as he was speaking with me, I was in a deep sleep with my face to the ground; but he touched me, and stood me upright. And he said, "Look, I am making known to you what shall happen in the latter time of the indignation; for at the appointed time the end *shall be.*

a. **Between the banks of the Ulai**: Daniel was still in the midst of his vision when he saw himself on the shores of this Persian river. He heard someone instruct **Gabriel** to explain the vision to Daniel.

b. **The vision refers to the time of the end**: Gabriel assured Daniel that this vision had to do with end times, with the **latter time of the indignation**.

i. This is a problem for some, because we see that the prophecy of Daniel 8:1-14 was fulfilled in the days of the Medo-Persian and Greek Empires, especially in the time of Antiochus Epiphanes. The terms **time of the end** and **latter time of the indignation** commonly refer to what we think of as the *end times*, not events fulfilled more than a 100 years before the birth of Jesus.

ii. The answer is that though this prophecy was fulfilled in Antiochus Epiphanes, it also has a later fulfillment in the Antichrist, referring to the **time of the end**. Antiochus Epiphanes is sometimes called the "Antichrist of the Old Testament." He prefigures the Antichrist of the end times.

iii. Just as Antiochus Epiphanes rose to power with force and intrigue, so will the Antichrist. As he persecuted the Jews, so will the Antichrist. As he stopped sacrifice and desecrated the temple, so will the Antichrist. As he seemed to be a complete success, so will the Antichrist. "From what Antiochus did to Jews in his day, therefore, one may know the

general pattern of what the Antichrist will do to them in the future."
(Wood)

iv. "Greece with all its refinement, culture and art, produced the Old
Testament Anti-Christ while the so called Christian nations produce
the New Testament Anti-Christ." (Heslop)

c. **What shall happen in the latter time of the indignation; for at
the appointed time the end**: Some see this Antiochus and Antichrist
connection, and some do not. Martin Luther wrote, "This chapter in
Daniel refers both to Antiochus and Antichrist." John Calvin wrote,
"Hence Luther, indulging his thoughts too freely, refers this passage to the
masks of Antichrist."

2. (20-22) The specific identification of the ram and the male goat of Daniel's
vision.

**The ram which you saw, having the two horns; *they are* the kings of
Media and Persia. And the male goat *is* the kingdom of Greece. The
large horn that *is* between its eyes *is* the first king. As for the broken
horn and the four that stood up in its place, four kingdoms shall arise
out of that nation, but not with its power.**

a. **The large horn that is between its eyes is the first king**: This was
fulfilled in history by Alexander the Great (see comments on Daniel 8:5-8).

b. **Four kingdoms shall arise out of that nation, but not with its power**:
This was fulfilled in history by the four generals who divided Alexander's
Empire between them (see comments on Daniel 8:5-8).

3. (23-26) The rise and fall of the strong little horn.

**"And in the latter time of their kingdom,
When the transgressors have reached their fullness,
A king shall arise,
Having fierce features,
Who understands sinister schemes.
His power shall be mighty, but not by his own power;
He shall destroy fearfully,
And shall prosper and thrive;
He shall destroy the mighty, and *also* the holy people.
"Through his cunning
He shall cause deceit to prosper under his rule;
And he shall exalt *himself* in his heart.
He shall destroy many in *their* prosperity.
He shall even rise against the Prince of princes;
But he shall be broken without *human* means.**

"And the vision of the evenings and mornings
Which was told is true;
Therefore seal up the vision,
For *it refers* to many days *in the future*."

a. **In the latter time of their kingdom**: The prophecy in this passage reads equally true of both Antiochus and Antichrist. This is an example of a prophetic passage that has both a *near* and *far* fulfillment.

b. **Having fierce features**: Antiochus Epiphanes was known for his cruel brutality. This will also be true of the coming Antichrist.

c. **Who understands sinister schemes... through his cunning**: Antiochus was known for his flattery and smooth tongue. The coming Antichrist will strike a covenant with Israel (Daniel 9:27).

d. **His power shall be mighty, but not by his own power**: Antiochus Epiphanes was empowered by Satan and allowed by God. The same will be true of the coming Antichrist.

e. **Shall prosper and thrive**: Antiochus Epiphanes looked like a total success. The coming Antichrist will look like a complete winner until God topples his reign.

f. **He shall destroy the mighty, and also the holy people**: Antiochus Epiphanes not only destroyed his enemies, but also harshly persecuted the people of God. The coming Antichrist will also destroy and persecute.

g. **He shall cause deceit to prosper**: Both the rule of Antiochus Epiphanes in the past and of the Antichrist in the future are marked by **deceit**. *The coming of the lawless one is according to the working of Satan, with all power, signs, and lying wonders, and with all unrighteous deception among those who perish, because they did not receive the love of the truth, that they might be saved* (2 Thessalonians 2:9-10).

h. **He shall exalt himself in his heart**: The coins of Antiochus Epiphanes were inscribed with this title: THEOS EPIPHANIES meaning, "God manifest." The coming Antichrist will also exalt himself: *So that he sits as God in the temple of God, showing himself that he is God* (2 Thessalonians 2:4).

i. **He shall even rise against the Prince of princes**: Though Antiochus Epiphanes hated the people of God and fought against them, it was because he really hated God. The same will be true of the coming Antichrist, who will hate the Jews because he hates God.

j. **Broken without human means**: History tells us that Antiochus Epiphanes died of disease, not by the hand of man. In a similar way no *man* will defeat the coming Antichrist, but the hand of Jesus will strike him down (Revelation 19:20).

k. **Therefore seal up the vision**: Daniel must do this because in his day the vision referred to a period far distant in its ultimate fulfillment. For us, the time is near (Revelation 1:3) and the book is unsealed (Revelation 22:10).

4. (27) Daniel reacts to the vision with physical shock and astonishment.

And I, Daniel, fainted and was sick for days; afterward I arose and went about the king's business. I was astonished by the vision, but no one understood it.

a. **Fainted and was sick... I was astonished**: Daniel probably couldn't understand why God would allow such a mighty persecutor of His people to come to power and seeming success.

i. "He may well have been puzzled about why Yahweh would permit even this brief time of brutal oppression under the little horn." (Archer)

b. **I went about the king's business**: Daniel didn't let either spiritual mysteries or physical weakness keep him from doing his duty. This shows us that our interest in prophecy should make us *more* concerned with our **king's business**, not *less* concerned about it.

i. "He would have counted it a great slur on his religious life if it could have been said that his visions and exercises interfered with his service to the king." (Meyer)

ii. "Let us not neglect the work of the Lord, though less able to perform it. A sick child's service is doubly accepted." (Trapp)

c. **No one understood it**: It wasn't because God never wanted this prophecy to be understood. There is no reason for God to reveal something to man that can never be understood. The reason why **no one understood it** was because the vision was sealed up in light of its ultimate fulfillment in Daniel's distant future.

i. It is worth repeating: the time is *not* distant for us in light of Revelation 1:3, and the book of prophecy is not sealed in light of Revelation 22:10.

Daniel 9 - The Seventy Weeks of Daniel

A. The prayer of Daniel.

1. (1-2) Introduction: Daniel's reason for prayer.

In the first year of Darius the son of Ahasuerus, of the lineage of the Medes, who was made king over the realm of the Chaldeans; in the first year of his reign I, Daniel, understood by the books the number of the years *specified* by the word of the LORD through Jeremiah the prophet, that He would accomplish seventy years in the desolations of Jerusalem.

a. **Understood by the books**: Daniel 9 is one of the most amazing and significant prophetic passages in the Bible, and it begins with Daniel's understanding and application of prophecy.

i. Daniel **understood** something from reading the words of God's prophets. Prophecy is meant to be **understood** - perhaps not in every detail, but certainly in its main points.

ii. Daniel understood this **by the books** - the *specific words* recorded in *God-inspired* **books**. Daniel couldn't read 2 Timothy 3:16, but he did believe the truth of it: *All Scripture is given by inspiration of God, and is profitable for doctrine, for reproof, for correction, for instruction in righteousness.*

iii. "These verses show Daniel as a diligent student of Scripture who built his prayer life on the Word of God." (Archer)

iv. "Oh! That you studied your Bibles more! Oh! That we all did! How we could plead the promises! How often we should prevail with God when we could hold him to his word, and say, 'Fulfill this word unto thy servant, whereon thou hast caused me to hope.' Oh! It is grand praying when our mouth is full of God's word, for there is no word that can prevail with him like his own." (Spurgeon)

93

b. **The number of years specified by the word of the LORD through Jeremiah**: Daniel knew that effective prayer comes out of knowing and praying both God's word and our present circumstances. His study of prophecy showed him a *specific number* - the 70 years described in Jeremiah 25:11-13 and Jeremiah 29:10, and his knowledge of the times led him to know those passages applied to his time.

> i. *"And this whole land shall be a desolation and an astonishment, and these nations shall serve the king of Babylon seventy years. 'Then it will come to pass, when seventy years are completed, that I will punish the king of Babylon and that nation, the land of the Chaldeans, for their iniquity,"* says the LORD; *"and I will make it a perpetual desolation. So I will bring on that land all My words which I have pronounced against it, all that is written in this book, which Jeremiah has prophesied concerning all the nations"* (Jeremiah 25:11-13).

> ii. *For thus says the LORD: After seventy years are completed at Babylon, I will visit you and perform My good word toward you, and cause you to return to this place* (Jeremiah 29:10).

> iii. It is important to note that Daniel regarded these as *real, literal years*. They were in no way understood as symbolic years.

> iv. Daniel was undoubtedly also familiar with Isaiah's prophecies concerning Cyrus (Isaiah 44:28-45:4). He must have been encouraged to see a man named Cyrus rise in power over Persia.

c. **That He would accomplish seventy years**: Daniel believed that God **would accomplish seventy years** of captivity, yet he prayed passionately that God would do what He promised to do. Daniel knew that God's promises *invite* our prayers and participation. They do not *exclude* our prayers and participation.

> i. "Nothing, therefore, can be better for us, than to ask for what he has promised." (Calvin)

> ii. This principle is repeated in many passages. 2 Peter 3:12 indicates that there is a sense in which we can *hasten* the Lord's coming by our holy conduct and godly lives; we can also hasten the Lord's coming through evangelism because Paul says that God's prophetic focus on Israel will resume when the *fullness of the Gentiles has come in* (Romans 11:25). This means that we can also hasten the Lord's coming through prayer, even as Daniel asked for a speedy fulfillment of prophecy regarding captive Israel (Daniel 9). We can also pray *Even so, come, Lord Jesus!* (Revelation 22:20). If we want Jesus to come soon, there is something we can *do* about it.

iii. But a second important reason is that Daniel asked God, in His mercy, to take the earliest of all possible starting points (Daniel's abduction) for determining the beginning of the 70 years. There were three waves of captivity:

- 605 B.C. - Jerusalem was attacked and Daniel and other captives were taken to Babylon.
- 597 B.C. - Jerusalem was attacked and treasure was taken from the temple.
- 587 B.C. - Jerusalem falls and the nation was exiled.

iv. Daniel wanted to prevail in prayer, asking God to take the earliest possible starting point to determine the 70 years. He wanted God's mercy to come to Israel 18 years earlier rather than 18 years later.

d. **In the first year of Darius**: This was still three or four years before 70 years had passed from 605 B.C. This was not too soon for Daniel to begin praying. Daniel had the foresight to look ahead three or four years and to begin praying.

e. **The word of the LORD through Jeremiah**: Even in God's eternal decrees, God has an essential role for people to play. God's plan of the ages is declared, yet Jeremiah made a prophecy; Daniel made a prayer, and Cyrus made a proclamation

i. "Too often our interest in the prophetic Scriptures is of a curious and speculative nature, or else we conclude that God will carry out His sovereign purpose no matter what we do, and so we do not concern ourselves with those matters." (Strauss)

ii. By his tribal heritage or family history Daniel was not uniquely qualified for a ministry of intercession. He did not belong to a priestly family like Ezekiel and he wasn't a career prophet like Isaiah or Jeremiah. Yet like all of us, he could pray.

iii. In fact, Daniel's calling and station in life made it *less* likely that he would be such a man of prayer. He was a high government official who almost certainly had a busy schedule - yet he took time and energy to pray.

iv. "Do not, I pray you, get into the habit of neglecting the assembling of yourselves together for prayer. How often have I said, 'All our strength lies in prayer'! When we were very few, God multiplied us in answer to prayer." (Spurgeon)

2. (3) Daniel's preparation for prayer.

Then I set my face toward the Lord God to make request by prayer and supplications, with fasting, sackcloth, and ashes.

a. **I set my face**: This implies *determination* in prayer. Daniel had a goal to reach through prayer, and he approached God as a man who would not be denied. He did this because he was rightly convinced that his prayer was in the will of God, and knew it was not motivated by any selfish desire.

b. **To make request by prayer and supplications**: Daniel wasn't *passive* as God's prophetic plan unfolded before him. In his approach to God he made a **request**, *asking* God to perform His promise in the way that Daniel thought would bring God most glory.

i. "We ask but little, and God gives it." (Spurgeon)

c. **With fasting, sackcloth, and ashes**: This reflected Daniel's humble heart in approaching God. **Fasting, sackcloth, and ashes** are emblems of humiliation and mourning.

i. Daniel was determined to do whatever it took to get this job done in prayer. He "left nothing undone that might possibly make his prayer more effective or more persuasive." (Walvoord)

3. (4-15) Daniel confesses the sin of his people, and glorifies the goodness and righteousness of God.

And I prayed to the LORD my God, and made confession, and said, "O Lord, great and awesome God, who keeps His covenant and mercy with those who love Him, and with those who keep His commandments, we have sinned and committed iniquity, we have done wickedly and rebelled, even by departing from Your precepts and Your judgments. Neither have we heeded Your servants the prophets, who spoke in Your name to our kings and our princes, to our fathers and all the people of the land. O Lord, righteousness *belongs* to You, but to us shame of face, as *it is* this day; to the men of Judah, to the inhabitants of Jerusalem and all Israel, those near and those far off in all the countries to which You have driven them, because of the unfaithfulness which they have committed against You. O Lord, to us *belongs* shame of face, to our kings, our princes, and our fathers, because we have sinned against You. To the Lord our God *belong* mercy and forgiveness, though we have rebelled against Him. We have not obeyed the voice of the LORD our God, to walk in His laws, which He set before us by His servants the prophets. Yes, all Israel has transgressed Your law, and has departed so as not to obey Your voice; therefore the curse and the oath written in the Law of Moses the servant of God have been poured out on us,

because we have sinned against Him. And He has confirmed His words, which He spoke against us and against our judges who judged us, by bringing upon us a great disaster; for under the whole heaven such has never been done as what has been done to Jerusalem. As *it is* written in the Law of Moses, all this disaster has come upon us; yet we have not made our prayer before the LORD our God, that we might turn from our iniquities and understand Your truth. Therefore the LORD has kept the disaster in mind, and brought it upon us; for the LORD our God *is* righteous in all the works which He does, though we have not obeyed His voice. And now, O Lord our God, who brought Your people out of the land of Egypt with a mighty hand, and made Yourself a name, as *it is* this day; we have sinned, we have done wickedly!"

a. **O Lord, great and awesome God**: Daniel began his prayer where we all should - by recognizing the greatness and goodness of God. Sometimes we approach God as if He were a stingy person who must be persuaded to give us anything. But Daniel knew the problem was not with God. God **keeps His covenant and mercy with those who love Him**.

i. Daniel's prayer was remarkable for both its *understanding* and *earnestness*. Many pray with understanding but not earnestness; others are earnest but have no understanding in prayer. The two together are a powerful combination.

ii. "Oh! That our prayers could get beyond praying, till they got to agonizing." (Spurgeon)

b. **We have sinned and committed iniquity**: As Daniel confessed Israel's sin he prayed as if he were as bad as the rest of Israel. This was a confession of **we**, not *they*. In this sense, *they* prayers never really reach God; genuine **we** prayers see self correctly and see our fellow saints with compassion.

i. Daniel's confession of sin might seem phony until we realize how passionately and completely he is focused on God. Compared to God, even the most righteous among us falls far short.

ii. "I firmly believe that, the better a man's own character becomes, and the more joy in the Lord he has in his own heart, the more capable is he of sympathetic sorrow; and, probably, the more of it he will have. If thou hast room in thy soul for sacred joy, thou hast equal room for holy grief." (Spurgeon)

c. **Righteousness belongs to You, but to us shame of face**: Daniel knew that Israel's sin was not God's fault; God was utterly righteous and blameless. Any **shame of face** belonged to Israel, not to God.

i. It would be easy to *complain* to God about Israel's problems. Daniel didn't think for a moment that God was too hard on Israel; he knew God was completely righteous and any failure was on Israel's side.

ii. Instead of *complaining*, Daniel *confessed*. During times of great revival among God's people, the Holy Spirit always brings a deep conviction and awareness of sin. When that is responded to rightly, confession is appropriately made. J. Edwin Orr gives a good principle to govern confession: "If you sin secretly, confess secretly, admitting publicly that you need the victory but keeping details to yourself. If you sin openly confess openly to remove stumbling blocks from those whom you have hindered. If you have sinned spiritually (prayerlessness, lovelessness, and unbelief as well as their offspring, criticism, etc.) then confess to the church that you have been a hindrance."

iii. Genuine, appropriate confession will be sincere, specific, and thorough. Orr describes how in the 1952 revival in Brazil a woman in a crowded church confessed, "Please pray for me, I need to love people more." The leader told her gently, "That is not a confession, sister. Anyone could have said it." Later in the service the lady stood again and said, "Please pray for me. What I should have said is that my sharp tongue has caused a lot of trouble in this congregation." The pastor leaned over to Orr and whispered, "Now she is talking!"

iv. This is praying from a low place, and very effective. Football players try to hit their opponent *low*, because they gain leverage from coming in low. Our prayers are leveraged when we come to God humbly and lowly.

d. **We have not obeyed the voice of the LORD our God**: Daniel did not make the slightest excuse for Israel's sin. He knew the fault belonged to Israel and Israel alone. We are prone to make excuses for our sin and often even make excuses in our "confessions."

e. **He has confirmed His words... As it is written in the Law of Moses**: Daniel realized that even in His judgment against Israel, God was totally faithful to His Word. He promised that curses would come upon a disobedient Israel (in passages like Leviticus 26 and Deuteronomy 28) and they did.

f. **All this disaster has come upon us; yet we have not made our prayer before the LORD our God**: As Daniel confessed his sin and the sin of Israel, he remembered the sin of *prayerlessness*. Even when they faced great trial and calamity, Israel still did not make their **prayer before the LORD**. When we sense trial or difficulty, it should drive us *immediately* to prayer - when we are not so driven, it should be a wake-up call to the coldness of our heart.

g. **Who brought Your people out of the land of Egypt with a mighty hand**: As Daniel prayed he remembered that the LORD delivered Israel from Egypt. He remembers the Old Testament standard of God's power, the deliverance from Egypt. The New Testament standard of God's power is the resurrection of Jesus (Ephesians 1:19-20).

4. (16-19) Daniel asks God to forgive and to restore Jerusalem.

"O Lord, according to all Your righteousness, I pray, let Your anger and Your fury be turned away from Your city Jerusalem, Your holy mountain; because for our sins, and for the iniquities of our fathers, Jerusalem and Your people *are* a reproach to all *those* around us. Now therefore, our God, hear the prayer of Your servant, and his supplications, and for the Lord's sake cause Your face to shine on Your sanctuary, which is desolate. O my God, incline Your ear and hear; open Your eyes and see our desolations, and the city which is called by Your name; for we do not present our supplications before You because of our righteous deeds, but because of Your great mercies. O Lord, hear! O Lord, forgive! O Lord, listen and act! Do not delay for Your own sake, my God, for Your city and Your people are called by Your name."

a. **Let Your anger and Your fury be turned away from Your city Jerusalem**: After his confession of Israel's sin and God's great righteousness, Daniel simply asked God to mercifully turn His kind attention to Jerusalem and the temple (**cause Your face to shine on Your sanctuary**). He also asked that God would do this without delay (**do not delay for your own sake**).

i. Daniel prayed as a patriot - but a patriot more of the Kingdom of God than the Kingdom of Israel. We should pray with similar patriotism for the Kingdom of God. "Let it never be said that the Church of God has no feeling of patriotism for the Holy City, for the Heavenly Land and for her glorious King enthroned above. To us, Christian patriotism means love to the Church of God." (Spurgeon)

ii. Daniel asked for all this **according to all Your righteousness**. It was as if Daniel prayed, "LORD, I'm not asking You to do anything against Your righteousness. I'm praying this to advance Your righteous glory."

b. **Cause your face to shine**: This was the heart of Daniel's plea. He knew that God's people needed much, but all their need could be summed up in this: *they need God's face to shine upon them.*

i. "Oh, that we might learn how to pray so that God should be the subject as well as the object of our supplications! O God, thy Church needs thee above everything else! A poor, little, sick, neglected child needs fifty things; but you can put all those needs into one if you say that the child needs its mother. So, the Church, of God needs a thousand things, but you can put them all into one if you say, 'The Church of God needs her God.' " (Spurgeon)

c. **For the Lord's sake cause Your face to shine on Your sanctuary, which is desolate... Do not delay for Your own sake**: Daniel's prayer was consumed with the glory of God, not primarily with the benefit of man. His purpose in prayer was to see God's work accomplished and His cause glorified.

i. It isn't wrong to pray for our own needs. Jesus invited us to ask, *give us this day our daily bread.* At the same time, we need to have an even greater passion for the glory and benefit of God than for our own needs.

ii. This also speaks to *purity of motive* in Daniel's prayer. Sometimes we pray for God to do a great work so we can be known as great workers for God. We need to pray for the sake of the LORD's cause, both in our words and heart.

d. **We do not present our supplications before You because of our righteous deeds, but because of Your great mercies**: Even before the time of the New Testament, Daniel prayed on firm New Testament ground. His confidence wasn't in *his* goodness, but in *God's* goodness.

i. This is what it means to pray *in the name of Jesus.* Those aren't words we tack on to the end of a prayer, but they should express the fact we are praying in merits and righteousness of Jesus, not our own.

ii. Daniel was not great because he prayed. He was great because his prayer was the necessary expression of great trust and dependence on God. Many religious people spend countless hours in prayer but it achieves *nothing* because it is not rooted in the goodness and righteousness of God. *Self righteous* or *self trusting* prayer is of no power before God. "One of Satan's most subtle delusions is that he succeeds in getting hundreds of thousands of men to trust in prayer, apart from faith in the shed blood of Jesus." (Talbot)

e. **O Lord, hear! O Lord, forgive! O Lord, listen and act!** Daniel prayed like a great wrestler, eager to gain an advantage. He sensed God's openness to each request and he responded with many rapid requests.

i. "Follow up your advantage; build another prayer or the answer that you have. If you have received a great blessing, say, 'Because he hath inclined his ear unto me, therefore will I call upon him; because he has heard me once, therefore will I call again.' " (Spurgeon)

ii. "Cold prayers ask God to deny them: only importunate prayers will be replied to. When the Church of God cannot take 'No' for an answer, she shall not have 'No' for an answer. When a pleading soul must have it; when the Spirit of God works mightily in him so that he cannot let the angel go without a blessing, the angel shall not go till he has given the blessing to such a pleading one. Brethren, if there be only one among us that can pray as Daniel did, with intensity, the blessing will come." (Spurgeon)

B. Gabriel brings the answer to Daniel's prayer.

1. (20-21) Daniel's prayer is interrupted by an angelic visit.

Now while I *was* speaking, praying, and confessing my sin and the sin of my people Israel, and presenting my supplication before the LORD my God for the holy mountain of my God, yes, while I *was* speaking in prayer, the man Gabriel, whom I had seen in the vision at the beginning, being caused to fly swiftly, reached me about the time of the evening offering.

a. **While I was speaking in prayer**: This dramatic answer to prayer came even as Daniel prayed. Jesus said, *your Father knows the things you have need of before you ask Him* (Matthew 6:8). Whenever there seems to be a delay in answer to prayer, there is reason for the delay. When it is right to do it, God can answer prayer immediately.

i. Sometimes God answers prayer even *before* we pray. *It shall come to pass that before they call, I will answer; and while they are still speaking, I will hear* (Isaiah 65:24).

b. **Being caused to fly swiftly**: This is one of the few places in the Bible where we are told that angels fly. Gabriel came quickly because there is no great distance between heaven and earth.

c. **The time of the evening offering**: This was a special time of day, when Moses offered the Passover lamb (Exodus 12:6) and when Jesus was crucified (Matthew 27:45).

i. As a young man in Jerusalem, Daniel often saw the smoke rising from the temple at the time of the evening sacrifice.

2. (22-23) Gabriel announces that he has come to bring Daniel an answer to his prayer.

And he informed *me*, and talked with me, and said, "O Daniel, I have now come forth to give you skill to understand. At the beginning of your

supplications the command went out, and I have come to tell *you*, for you *are* greatly beloved; therefore consider the matter, and understand the vision:"

a. **I have now come forth to give you skill to understand**: In his prayer, Daniel didn't ask for understanding. His prayer demonstrated that his heart was close to God's heart, so as a friend, God revealed many things to Daniel (John 15:15).

i. Daniel studied the passage in Jeremiah, but still didn't understand much. In this case, understanding came more through *prayer*. "All students of the word will tell you that when the hammers of learning and biblical criticism have failed to break open a flinty text, oftentimes prayer has done it, and nuggets of gold have been found concealed therein. To every student of the word of God who would become a well-instructed scribe we would say, with all the means which you employ, with all your searchings of the commentaries, with all your diggings into the original, with all your researches among learned divines, mingle much fervent prayer." (Spurgeon)

ii. "Luther affirmeth that he oft got more spiritual light by some... ardent prayer than ever he could do by the reading of many books, or by the most accurate meditation thereupon." (Trapp)

b. **For you are greatly beloved**: Both Daniel and the Apostle John (John 13:23) were noted for their love-relationship with God. Both Daniel and John were also noted for receiving amazing prophetic messages.

i. Daniel had just considered a set of "sevens" upon the nation of Israel - the 70 years of promised captivity prophesied by Jeremiah. It was as if God said through Gabriel, "Now I will show you some 'sevens' that will really amaze you."

ii. Daniel illustrated the principle that when we seek God diligently, we often receive even more than we ask for.

C. The prophecy of the Seventy Weeks.

1. (24a) **Seventy weeks** are determined for the Jews and Jerusalem.

**"Seventy weeks are determined
For your people and for your holy city,**

a. **Seventy weeks are determined**: There is almost universal agreement among Bible scholars and commentators that this refers to **seventy** sets of seven years, or *weeks of years*.

i. In ancient Hebrew, **weeks** simply refers to a unit of seven. The Hebrew word here is often used to mean a unit of seven days, but it may also be used for a unit of seven years.

ii. "The Jews had *Sabbatic years*, by which their years were divided into weeks of years, as in this important prophecy, each week containing *seven* years." (Clarke)

iii. Genesis 29:15-28 is an example of using this ancient Hebrew word (*shabuwa*) for both seven days and seven years in the same context.

b. **For your people and for your holy city**: The seventy weeks were focused upon Daniel's **people** (the Jews) and his **holy city** (Jerusalem).

i. Unless the church has become Israel, it is not in view here. Talbot calls the seventy weeks "God's calendar for Israel" in the sense that it does not focus on the Gentiles or the church.

2. (24b) What will be accomplished in the seventy weeks.

To finish the transgression,
To make an end of sins,
To make reconciliation for iniquity,
To bring in everlasting righteousness,
To seal up vision and prophecy,
And to anoint the Most Holy.

a. **To finish the transgression**: This says that transgression itself will be finished. Taken literally, this means establishing an entirely new order on earth, with an end to man's rebellion against God.

i. "The culmination of appointed years will witness the conclusion of man's 'transgression' or 'rebellion' against God - a development most naturally entered into with the establishment of an entirely new order on earth. This seems to require nothing less than the inauguration of the kingdom of God on earth." (Archer)

b. **To make an end of sins**: Taking these words at face value, this means not only the **end** of the guilt of sin, but an **end** of sin itself. It means to "seal up" or to "restrain" sins. This looks to a new, redeemed world.

c. **To make reconciliation for iniquity**: Man's **iniquity** must be reconciled to God's justice and holiness. This work was clearly accomplished at the cross.

d. **To bring in everlasting righteousness**: One might take this in an individual sense, but there have always been righteous *individuals*. Taking the statement at face value, this means a new order of society brought in by the Messiah.

e. **To seal up vision and prophecy**: This speaks of both the ending and fulfillment of prophecy, concluding the final stage of human history and culminating with the reign of the Son of God.

> i. "It must include his enthronement." (Archer)

f. **To anoint the most holy**: Taken at its simple, literal meaning, this refers to a place, not a person. There is a **most holy** place - the **most holy** place of the temple - that will be anointed and blessed.

> i. Taken as a whole, Gabriel made a remarkable announcement to Daniel. He told him that each of these amazing things would happen within the period of **seventy weeks**.

> ii. Looking back in history, we can only say these things are *already* fulfilled if we ignore their plain, literal meaning and give them a spiritualized meaning that replaces their plain meaning. Some believe that these promises were fulfilled generally in the spread of the Gospel over the centuries, but this belief neglects the plain and simple meaning of these words.

3. (25) The course and dividing of the seventy weeks.

"Know therefore and understand,
That **from the going forth of the command**
To restore and build Jerusalem
Until Messiah the Prince,
There shall be **seven weeks and sixty-two weeks;**
The street shall be built again, and the wall,
Even in troublesome times.

a. **From the going forth of the command to restore and build Jerusalem**: Here Gabriel revealed to Daniel the *starting point* for the seventy-weeks prophecy. There was a **command to restore and build Jerusalem** in history that started this specific period of time.

> i. The Bible presents four possible decrees that might fulfill this description:

> > • Cyrus made a decree giving Ezra and the Babylonian captives the right to return to Jerusalem and rebuild the temple in 538 B.C. (Ezra 1:1-4 and 5:13-17).

> > • Darius made a decree giving Ezra the right to rebuild the temple in 517 B.C. (Ezra 6:6-12).

> > • Artaxerxes made a decree giving Ezra permission, safe passage, and supplies to return to Jerusalem to rebuild the temple in 458 B.C. (Ezra 7:11-26).

- Artaxerxes made a decree giving Nehemiah permission, safe passage and supplies to return to Jerusalem to rebuild the city and the walls in 445 B.C. (Nehemiah 2:1-8).

ii. Only the last of these four decrees was a **command to restore and build Jerusalem**. The first three each focused on the *temple*, not on **the street** or on **the wall**.

b. **Until Messiah the Prince, there shall be seven weeks and sixty-two weeks**: Gabriel's message to Daniel was simple and striking. 483 years - that is, 69 units of seven years - would pass from the time of the command recorded in Nehemiah 2:1-8 until the appearance of **Messiah the Prince**.

i. Some say the 483 years were completed at the time of Jesus' birth (5 or 4 B.C.). There is little chronological support for this date.

ii. Some say the 483 years were completed at His baptism, at the beginning of Jesus' ministry (if dated at A.D. 26). This is possible if one begins with the earlier decree of Artaxerxes, and figures with our present measurement for years (365.25 days to a year) instead of the ancient measurement of years (360 days to a year).

iii. Some say the 483 years were completed at the triumphal entry of Jesus (if dated at A.D. 32). Sir Robert Anderson's significant work *The Coming Prince* followed this argument in great detail.

- Anderson, using a 360-day year (which Israel used in Daniel's day), calculated 173,880 days from the decree to the triumphal entry, fulfilling the prophecy *to the day*. "It is customary for the Jews to have twelve months of 360 days each and then to insert a thirteenth month occasionally when necessary to correct the calendar." (Walvoord)

- The year A.D. 32 (based on Luke 3:1) for Jesus' death is controversial (most chronologists favor A.D. 30 or 33). But recent attempts have made some case for the date: "A recent article attempts to give credence to the date of A.D. 32; cf. R.E. Showers, *Grace Journal*, XI (Winter, 1970), pp. 30ff. The evidence presented is worthy of notice." (Wood)

- "No one today is able dogmatically to declare that Sir Robert Anderson's computations are impossible." (Walvoord)

iv. Some say the 483 years were completed at the exact time of the crucifixion. This is a minority opinion. Most who find the date near this time also see it belonging to the Triumphal Entry, which happened seven days before the crucifixion.

c. **Until Messiah the Prince**: Taking Anderson's calculations as reliable, we see a *remarkable* fulfillment of prophecy. A Gentile king made a decree and 483 years later *to the day*, Jesus presented Himself as **Messiah the Prince** to Israel.

i. In our mind a **Prince** is a good step lower than a *king*. In the Hebrew vocabulary, "**Prince**" has more the idea of "strong, mighty ruler" than "son of a king and heir to the throne."

ii. "There was only one occasion in our Lord's earthly ministry on which He is depicted as presenting Himself openly as Zion's King, the so-called 'Triumphal Entry,' recorded in each one of the Gospels and fulfilling Zechariah 9:9 and Psalm 118:26." (Newell)

- On that day, Jesus *deliberately* arranged the event to present Himself as Messiah (Mark 11:1-10).
- On that day, Jesus welcomed praise (Luke 19:38-40) instead of quieting it (Luke 5:14 and 8:56).
- On that day, Jesus made special reference to the importance of that day (Luke 19:41-42).

iii. This prophecy is so specifically fulfilled that it has been a significant testimony to many. "Others of the Jewish [scholars], by the evidence of these words, have been compelled to confess that Messiah is already come, and that he was that Jesus whom their forefathers crucified." (Trapp)

d. **The street shall be built again, and the wall, even in troublesome times**: This indicates that the rebuilding of the streets and wall of Jerusalem would happen in the first **seven weeks** mentioned. Then would follow another 62 weeks of years until the coming of **Messiah the Prince**.

i. The seventy weeks are divided into three parts:

- Seven weeks - 49 years, until the city and its walls are rebuilt.
- 69 weeks (7 plus 62), 483 years from the decree, until Messiah the Prince appears.
- A final 70th week to complete the prophecy.

4. (26) What happens after the first sixty-nine weeks.

"And after the sixty-two weeks
Messiah shall be cut off, but not for Himself;
And the people of the prince who is to come
Shall destroy the city and the sanctuary.

The end of it *shall be* with a flood,
And till the end of the war desolations are determined.

a. **After the sixty-two weeks Messiah shall be cut off**: The Biblical term **cut off** is sometimes used to describe execution (see Genesis 9:11 and Exodus 31:14). Gabriel told Daniel that the Messiah will **be cut off** for the sake of others, **not for Himself**.

i. "Able chronologists have shown that the crucifixion of the Lord Jesus Christ occurred immediately after the expiration of 483 prophetic years, of 360 days each, from the time of Artaxerxes' order." (Ironside)

ii. Strangely, many able commentators simply ignore these numbers. "The numbers are symbolic and not arithmetical." (Baldwin)

iii. **Cut off** is a poignant description of Jesus' earthly life up to and including the cross. "Born in another man's stable, cradled in another man's manger with nowhere to lay his head during his life on earth, and buried in another man's tomb after dying on a cursed cross, the Christ of God and the Friend of the friendless was indeed cut off and had nothing." (Heslop)

b. **Shall destroy the city and the sanctuary**: After the Messiah was **cut off**, Jerusalem and her temple would be destroyed *again* by an overwhelming army (**with a flood**). Most all Bible scholars and commentators agree that this was fulfilled in the Roman destruction of Jerusalem in A.D. 70.

c. **The people of the prince who is to come shall destroy**: The destroying army is made up of the **people of the prince who is to come**. This *coming prince* is described more in Daniel 9:26.

5. (27) The events of the seventieth week.

Then he shall confirm a covenant with many for one week;
But in the middle of the week
He shall bring an end to sacrifice and offering.
And on the wing of abominations shall be one who makes desolate,
Even until the consummation, which is determined,
Is poured out on the desolate."

a. **He shall confirm a covenant**: The "he" Gabriel described is the *prince who is to come* mentioned in the previous verse. If we know that the prince's *people* destroyed Jerusalem in A.D. 70, then we know this coming prince has his ancestral roots in the soil of the ancient Roman Empire.

i. Therefore, the *prince who is to come* will in some way be an heir to the Romans, even as the final world government is an heir to the Roman Empire (Daniel 7).

b. **He shall confirm a covenant with many for one week**: The coming prince will make a **covenant** with Israel for the final unit of seven years, completing the seventy weeks prophesied for the Jewish people and Jerusalem.

i. **Covenant with many**: The word **many** here is a *specific* reference to Israel, not a *general* reference to a group. The ancient Hebrew says, "*covenant with the many.*"

ii. With this **covenant** Israel will embrace the Antichrist as a political messiah, if not the literal Messiah. Jesus predicted this in John 5:43: *I have come in My Father's name, and you do not receive Me; if another comes in his own name, him you will receive.*

iii. Taking the description of what would be accomplished in the 70 Weeks from Daniel 9:24, we know that the 70 Weeks are not yet complete. Yet the events promised in the first 69 weeks *are* fulfilled, indicated that there is a lengthy "pause" in the 70 Weeks, between the 69th week and the 70th week. The 70th week will begin when the coming prince **shall confirm a covenant** with the Jewish people. These gaps or pauses in prophecy may seem strange to us, but they are common. Comparing Isaiah 9:6 and Luke 1:31-33 shows another significant pause or gap in prophecy regarding the coming of the Messiah.

iv. We can think of it in this way: God appointed 490 years of special focus on Israel in His redemptive plan. The years were paused by Israel's rejection of Jesus. Now there is no *special* focus on Israel in God's redemptive plan because this is the time of the church. God's focus will return to Israel when the church is taken away (at the rapture) and the last seven years of man's rule on this earth begin.

v. "The 70th week will begin when the Jewish people are restored in unbelief to their land and city; and among them will be found a faithful remnant, owning their sin, and seeking Jehovah's face." (Henry Ironside writing in 1911)

c. **In the middle of the week he shall bring an end to sacrifice and offering**: The coming prince will break the covenant with Israel in the **middle** of the seven years, the final week (period of seven years).

i. The Book of Revelation sees this seven year period with both its halves as yet future (Revelation 12:6, 13-14; 13:5-9, 14-15). The **middle of the week** and the **end of sacrifice** had not yet happened in 90 A.D.

d. **On the wing of abominations shall be one who makes desolate**: The ending of sacrifice will come with **abominations**, followed by tremendous *desolation*.

    i. **Abominations** translates an ancient Hebrew word (*shiqquwts*) that is connected to horrific idolatry (Deuteronomy 29:17, 1 Kings 11:5-7, 2 Kings 23:13). The idea is that the coming prince breaks the covenant and brings an end to sacrifice and offering by desecrating the holy place of the temple with a horrific idolatry.

    ii. Jesus called this the *abomination of desolation* (Matthew 24:15) and indicated that it would be a pivotal sign in the Great Tribulation. Paul referred to the idolatry of the coming prince in 2 Thessalonians 2:3-4.

e. **Until the consummation, which is determined, is poured out on the desolate**: This breaking of the covenant and abomination of desolation has a promised **consummation**. Before the 70th week is completed, each of the things described in Daniel 9:24 will be accomplished and everlasting righteousness will reign.

The Seventy Weeks of Daniel
as Understood by Sir Robert Anderson in
"The Coming Prince"

Daniel 9:24-25 says that from the decree to rebuild Jerusalem to the coming of the Messiah there will be 483 years.

7 + 62 "weeks" = 69 groups of seven years. 7 x 69 = 483 years.

Anderson understood a prophetic year as 360 days. This is based both on ancient history and on Revelation 11:2, 13:5, 11:3, and 12:6 which indicate that 42 months - 3 ½ years - are equal to 1,260 days.

Therefore, 483 years x 360 days = **173,880** days.

Artaxerxes started his reign in 465 B.C. The decree to rebuild Jerusalem was given on the first day of Nisan, in the 20th year of Artaxerxes. In our calendar system (the Julian calendar) that date is March 14, 445 B.C. (Nehemiah 2:1)

Jesus started His ministry in the 15th year of Tiberius (see Luke 3:1). Tiberius started his reign in A.D. 14, so Jesus' ministry started in A.D. 29. Anderson believed that Jesus celebrated four Passovers during His ministry, one each in A.D. 29, 30, 31. and His final Passover in A.D. 32. With the help of lunar charts, we can calculate the exact date of ancient Passovers, so it is possible to calculate the exact day of Jesus' triumphal entry into Jerusalem as April 6, A.D. 32.

From 445 B.C. to A.D. 32. there are 476 years on the Julian calendar
(not 477 years, because there is no year zero).

476 years x 365 days = **173,740** days.

Adjusting for the difference between March 14 and April 6 adds **24** days.

Adjusting for leap years over a period of 476 years adds **116** days.

The total number of days from March 14, 445 B.C. to April 6, A.D. 32.

173,740 + 24 + 116 = 173,880 days.

According to his calendar, Daniel told us there would be **173,880** days between the decree and the arrival of Messiah the Prince. According to the calculations of Sir Robert Anderson, this was fulfilled precisely to the day.

Jesus said to the Jews of this day:

> *If you had known, even you, especially IN THIS YOUR DAY,*
> *the things that make for your peace!* (Luke 19:42).

David said of this day in Psalm 118:24:

> THIS IS THE DAY *which the Lord has made; we will rejoice and be glad in it.*

Daniel 10 - Circumstances of the Final Vision

A. Daniel's vision of the mysterious man.

1. (1-3) Introduction: Daniel's state of heart.

In the third year of Cyrus king of Persia a message was revealed to Daniel, whose name was called Belteshazzar. The message *was* true, but the appointed time *was* long; and he understood the message, and had understanding of the vision. In those days I, Daniel, was mourning three full weeks. I ate no pleasant food, no meat or wine came into my mouth, nor did I anoint myself at all, till three whole weeks were fulfilled.

a. **In the third year of Cyrus**: By this time, the first wave of exiles had returned under the leadership of Ezra (Ezra 1-2).

b. **The message was true, but the appointed time was long**: Daniel 10 sets the stage for the spectacular prophecy (**message**) of Daniel 11, which described a time of great persecution and testing for the people of Israel.

   i. Walvoord on **the appointed time was long**: "The implication is that the period in view is a long and strenuous one involving great conflict and trouble for the people of God."

c. **Mourning three full weeks**: Some think that Daniel was in mourning because so few Jews had returned with Ezra from exile. Others believe it was because Ezra faced severe opposition in rebuilding the temple.

   i. Daniel did not go back with Ezra's group of exiles because he was about 84 years old at this time. Daniel could serve the exiles better from his high position in government than he could with them in Jerusalem.

   ii. "I think too that Daniel's sorrow was occasioned partly by the repetition of those words to him: 'The vision is true, but the time appointed is long.' " (Spurgeon)

d. **I ate no pleasant food, no meat or wine came into my mouth**: It would be wrong to call what Daniel did fasting. The Biblical idea of fasting is to abstain from food altogether, drinking only water. Daniel definitely practiced a form of self-denial, but it was not fasting.

2. (4-6) Daniel sees a glorious man on the banks of the Tigris River.

Now on the twenty-fourth day of the first month, as I was by the side of the great river, that *is*, the Tigris, I lifted my eyes and looked, and behold, a certain man clothed in linen, whose waist *was* girded with gold of Uphaz! His body *was* like beryl, his face like the appearance of lightning, his eyes like torches of fire, his arms and feet like burnished bronze in color, and the sound of his words like the voice of a multitude.

a. **A certain man clothed in linen**: Commentators divide over the identity of this **certain man**. Some say this is Jesus, noting that the description is remarkably like what John saw in Revelation 1:12-16.

b. **A certain man clothed in linen**: Some others think that the **certain man** is an unnamed angel of high rank, noting that Jesus would not need the assistance of Michael, mentioned in Daniel 10:13.

i. We also know that Ezekiel saw angelic figures **clothed in linen** (Ezekiel 9:2).

3. (7) Daniel's companions are terrified, yet unseeing.

And I, Daniel, alone saw the vision, for the men who were with me did not see the vision; but a great terror fell upon them, so that they fled to hide themselves.

a. **I, Daniel, alone saw the vision**: This shows that there was something supernatural about this vision. Daniel saw what he saw regarding the glorious man, but his companions could not see it.

i. This is like the latter instance of Saul on the road to Damascus, when his companions could not hear the same voice from heaven that he heard. These cases remind us that we can be close to the presence and power of God, yet miss the message through lack of spiritual perception.

b. **They fled to hide themselves**: Of course they couldn't see the vision if they were hiding from it.

4. (8-9) Daniel's reaction to the sight of the man.

Therefore I was left alone when I saw this great vision, and no strength remained in me; for my vigor was turned to frailty in me, and I retained no strength. Yet I heard the sound of his words; and while I heard the

sound of his words I was in a deep sleep on my face, with my face to the ground.

a. **No strength remained in me**: As godly as Daniel was, he was undone by this vision of the glorious man. Daniel's experience shows us that even the holiest of men fall short before God and even before His closest associates.

b. **My vigor was turned to frailty**: Wood says of this word **frailty**, "The word suggests a death-like paleness, combined with a grotesque wrenching of facial features."

i. "To judge by the description, the trance experienced was not one to envy." (Baldwin)

B. The message to Daniel.

1. (10-11) The certain man introduces himself to Daniel.

Suddenly, a hand touched me, which made me tremble on my knees and *on* the palms of my hands. And he said to me, "O Daniel, man greatly beloved, understand the words that I speak to you, and stand upright, for I have now been sent to you." While he was speaking this word to me, I stood trembling.

a. **A hand touched me**: As Daniel was laid out in weakness by this experience, he was strengthened by the touch of **a hand**.

b. **O Daniel, man greatly beloved**: This was the second time Daniel was called **greatly beloved** (Daniel 9:23 previous to this). Each time it was in relation to Daniel's being favored with a great and significant revelation of the future.

i. "It did not do Daniel any harm to know that he was greatly beloved of God; or else he would not have received that information from heaven. Some people are always afraid that, if Christian people obtain full assurance, and receive a sweet sense of divine love, they will grow proud, and be carried away with conceit. Do not you have any such fear for other people, and especially do not be afraid of it for yourselves. I know of no greater blessing that can happen to any man and woman here, than to be assured by the Spirit of God that they are greatly beloved of the Lord." (Spurgeon)

c. **Stand upright**: When it was time for Daniel to hear and understand, he needed to **stand** at attention.

2. (12-14) The angel explains his coming to Daniel, and the opposition he faced on the way.

Then he said to me, "Do not fear, Daniel, for from the first day that you set your heart to understand, and to humble yourself before your God,

your words were heard; and I have come because of your words. But the prince of the kingdom of Persia withstood me twenty-one days; and behold, Michael, one of the chief princes, came to help me, for I had been left alone there with the kings of Persia. Now I have come to make you understand what will happen to your people in the latter days, for the vision *refers* to *many* days yet *to come.*"

a. **From the first day... your words were heard**: God responded to Daniel's prayer the very moment he made his request known. Daniel had been in great and serious prayer for *three full weeks* (Daniel 10:2).

b. **I have come because of your words**: We can't pass this over lightly. *An angel was dispatched because of Daniel's prayer.* This is another of many reminders in the Book of Daniel that prayer matters. It isn't merely a therapeutic exercise for the one who prays.

c. **The prince of the kingdom of Persia withstood me**: Since this **prince** was able to oppose the angelic messenger to Daniel, we know this was more than a man. This **prince** was some kind of angelic being, and we know he was an evil angelic being because he opposed the word of God coming to Daniel and stood against the angelic messenger.

i. The word **prince** has the idea of a ruler or authority. This fits in well with the New Testament idea that angelic ranks are organized and have a hierarchy (Ephesians 1:21, Ephesians 6:12, Colossians 1:16, Colossians 2:15). These angelic ranks seem to include both faithful angels and fallen angels.

ii. Apparently, this was a demon of high rank that opposed the answer to prayer. On three occasions, Jesus referred to Satan as *the prince of this world* (John 12:31, 14:30, and 16:11).

d. **Withstood me twenty-one days**: Since the angel was dispatched immediately and Daniel's period of prayer and self-denial was 21 days (the *three full weeks* of Daniel 10:2), we see that the answer to the prayer was delayed by **the prince of the kingdom of Persia**.

i. The correlation between Daniel's time of self-denial and prayer and the duration of the battle between the angels and the **prince of the kingdom of Persia** establishes a link between Daniel's prayer and the angelic victory. Since the angelic victory came on the 21ˢᵗ day, we can surmise that if Daniel would have stopped praying on the 20ᵗʰ day, the answer may not have come.

ii. "There may be hindering factors of which a praying Christian knows nothing as he wonders why the answers to his requests are delayed. Nevertheless, he is to keep on praying. It may be that he will not receive an answer because he has given up on the twentieth day when he should have persisted to the twenty-first day." (Archer)

e. **Michael, one of the chief princes, came to help me**: In other passages **Michael** is associated with the battle between good angels and evil angels (Revelation 12, Jude 9).

i. **Came to help me**: This phrase may be the most compelling reason to think that this "**me**" is not Jesus, despite the remarkable similarity between the *certain man* of Daniel 10 and the vision of Jesus in Revelation 1. Though Jesus received angelic assistance as an incarnate man (Mark 1:13 and Luke 22:43), it is difficult to think of Him needing or receiving angelic help before the incarnation.

f. **Now I have come**: God allowed this kind of conflict because He had a purpose in allowing it. He certainly *could have* blasted away in a moment any demonic opposition. God's plan probably was to use the time of delay to develop Daniel as a man of persistent prayer.

i. Persistence in prayer is not necessary because God's reluctance needs to be overcome; rather, it is necessary to train us.

ii. Daniel's success makes us reflect on our failures. How much angelic assistance or insight has never been realized, or greatly delayed, because of a lack of persistence in prayer?

g. **What will happen to your people in the latter days**: The vision of Daniel 11 and 12 was focused on the **latter days**, though it also relates to the closer time of Antiochus Epiphanes.

3. (15-19) Daniel is strengthened in his weakness.

When he had spoken such words to me, I turned my face toward the ground and became speechless. And suddenly, *one* having the likeness of the sons of men touched my lips; then I opened my mouth and spoke, saying to him who stood before me, "My lord, because of the vision my sorrows have overwhelmed me, and I have retained no strength. For how can this servant of my lord talk with you, my lord? As for me, no strength remains in me now, nor is any breath left in me." Then again, *the one* having the likeness of a man touched me and strengthened me. And he said, "O man greatly beloved, fear not! Peace *be* to you; be strong, yes, be strong!" So when he spoke to me I was strengthened, and said, "Let my lord speak, for you have strengthened me."

a. **I turned my face toward the ground and became speechless**: Daniel started on the ground (Daniel 10:9), then stood up (Daniel 10:11), and now was back on his **face** again.

b. **Because of the vision my sorrows have overwhelmed me**: The ancient Hebrew word translated **sorrows** has the thought of twisting or writhing pain. It is used in several places in the Old Testament for labor pains in childbirth. Daniel was so severely affected by this vision that he could barely breathe, much less could he deal with prophetic complexities.

c. **One having the likeness of a man touched me and strengthened me**: This was not God, but an angel. God touched Daniel through an intermediary.

4. (10:20-11:1) The angel introduces his message to Daniel.

Then he said, "Do you know why I have come to you? And now I must return to fight with the prince of Persia; and when I have gone forth, indeed the prince of Greece will come. But I will tell you what is noted in the Scripture of Truth. (No one upholds me against these, except Michael your prince. Also in the first year of Darius the Mede, I, *even* I, stood up to confirm and strengthen him)."

a. **I must return to fight with the prince of Persia**: Daniel was about to receive the answer to his prayer, but the battle was not over for his heavenly messenger. First he must battle **the prince of Persia**, then **the prince of Greece**. God watched out for Israel, working behind the scenes in the spiritual realm.

i. "The heavenly warfare is to be directed against first Persia and then Greece, because each of these in turn will have power over God's people." (Baldwin)

b. **No one upholds me against these, except Michael your prince**: Michael seemed to be an angelic guardian of Israel, battling against the demonic representative of Persia or any other who opposed God's people. On earth, Israel seemed lowly and weak; but in the heavens, Israel had the mightiest representative of all.

Daniel 11 - Antiochus and Antichrist Revisited

Introduction

1. This chapter contains one of the most specifically fulfilled prophecies of the Bible, predicting history over some 375 years, and to the end, with amazing accuracy.

2. The chapter is so specific, that many critics who deny supernatural revelation, have insisted that it is *history*, written after the fact, fraudulently claiming to be prophecy.

   a. Because of the detail of the prophecy, we will be forced to frequently summarize; and the fulfillment of the prophecy will be observed as it is described.

3. Commentator Joyce Baldwin explains the mindset of late-daters: "Though all of this is presented as if it were future, the considered opinion of most scholars is that the writer was using an accepted literary form, which would have deceived no-one. The intention would be to show that the course of history was under God's direction, and so achieving His purposes... When the history becomes prophecy the transition can be detected, because events proved him wrong."

   a. Such a view *must* undermine confidence in the entire book. If the late dating theory is correct, then "the so-called revelation was in fact nothing of the sort... it follows that the preparation for the vision in chapter 10 was also a fiction put in as local colour for the sake of effect." (Baldwin)

A. The division of the Greek Empire.

1. (2) Four future kings.

And now I will tell you the truth: Behold, three more kings will arise in Persia, and the fourth shall be far richer than *them* all; by his strength, through his riches, he shall stir up all against the realm of Greece.

   a. **Three more kings will arise in Persia**: Simply, the angel told Daniel that there would be three more kings **in Persia** until a fourth arose. The

fourth king would be strong, rich, and oppose **the realm of Greece**. This strong, rich **fourth** king was fulfilled in the Persian King Xerxes.

b. **The fourth shall be far richer**: In fulfillment, there were actually four kings from the time Daniel spoke of until Xerxes, the one who did **stir up all against the realm of Greece**. Either the angel omitted the current king (Cyrus), looking only to the future, or he ignored King Smerdis of Persia (522-21 B.C.) because he ruled less than one year and was an imposter to the throne.

c. **Persia... Greece**: These visions and insights regarding the future of the Persian and Greek Empires were relevant because each empire attempted to wipe out the people of God at some time.

> i. The Persian Empire tried to wipe out the Jewish people during the reign of Xerxes, through the plot of Haman (as shown in the Book of Esther).

> ii. The Greek Empire tried to wipe out the Jewish people during the reign of Antiochus IV, when he attempted to kill every Jew who did not renounce their commitment to God and embrace Greek culture.

2. (3-4) The rise of a mighty king.

Then a mighty king shall arise, who shall rule with great dominion, and do according to his will. And when he has arisen, his kingdom shall be broken up and divided toward the four winds of heaven, but not among his posterity nor according to his dominion with which he ruled; for his kingdom shall be uprooted, even for others besides these.

a. **Then a mighty king shall arise**: The angel told Daniel of a mighty king with a **great dominion** - but his kingdom would not endure, and it would be divided after the death of the **mighty king**.

b. **Shall rule with great dominion and do according to his will**: This was fulfilled in Alexander the Great, who certainly was **a mighty king**. Alexander died at 32 years of age of a fever after a drunken party in Babylon.

> i. This prophecy does not mainly concern Alexander because he did no harm to Jerusalem though he conquered the general area. The ancient historian Josephus records the interesting arrival of Alexander the Great to Jerusalem, and how he was shown the Book of Daniel by the high priest (whom Alexander had previously seen in a vision). Alexander was so impressed that he spared Jerusalem and granted it religious toleration (see Appendix B, page 141).

c. **Not among his posterity**: After Alexander's death, none of his descendants succeeded him. It wasn't for lack of trying. Alexander did leave three possible heirs: a half brother named Philip, who was mentally deficient; a son who was born after Alexander died; and an illegitimate son named Hercules. The half-brother and the posthumous son were first designated co-monarchs, each with a regent. But fighting amongst the regents eventually resulted in the murder of all possible heirs.

d. **Divided toward the four winds of heaven**: After the death of all Alexander's possible heirs, four generals controlled the Greek Empire, but none of them **according to his** (Alexander's) **dominion**.

i. The rest of this prophecy focuses on two of the four inheritors of Alexander's realm, and the dynasties they established. Only two are focused on because they constantly fought over the Promised Land because it sat between their centers of power.

B. The kings of the North and the kings of the South.

1. (5) The strength of the king of the South.

Also the king of the South shall become strong, as well as _one_ of his princes; and he shall gain power over him and have dominion. His dominion _shall be_ a great dominion.

a. **The king of the South shall become strong**: One of the four inheritors of the empire of the _mighty king_ would become stronger and greater than the others.

b. **He shall gain power over him and have dominion**: This was fulfilled in Ptolemy I of Egypt, who exerted his control over the Holy Land. Soon after the division of Alexander's Empire, the Ptolemies dominated this region.

i. Ptolemy I had a prince named Seleucus, who rose to power and took dominion over the region of Syria. He became more powerful than his former Egyptian ruler. The Seleucids are identified with the _Kings of the North_, and the Ptolemies were the _Kings of the South_.

ii. The dynasties of the Seleucids and the Ptolemies fought for some 130 years. The stronger of the two always held dominion over the Holy Land.

2. (6) A marriage between the families of the kings of the North and the kings of the South.

And at the end of _some_ years they shall join forces, for the daughter of the king of the South shall go to the king of the North to make an agreement; but she shall not retain the power of her authority, and neither he nor his authority shall stand; but she shall be given up, with those who brought her, and with him who begot her, and with him who strengthened her in _those_ times.

a. **They shall join forces**: Joined by a marriage, the kings of the North and South would be allies for a while, but the arrangement would not last.

b. **The daughter of the king of the South shall go to the king of the North to make an agreement**: This was fulfilled in the marriage between Antiochus II (of the Seleucids) and Berenice (daughter of Ptolemy II). There was peace for a time because of this marriage, but it was upset when Ptolemy II died.

> i. **Shall not retain the power of her authority**: Once Ptolemy II died, Antiochus II put away Berenice and took back his former wife, Laodice.

> ii. **Neither he nor his authority shall stand**: Laodice didn't trust her husband Antiochus II; so she had him poisoned.

> iii. **She shall be given up, with those who brought her**: After the murder of Antiochus II, Laodice had Berenice, her infant son, and her attendants killed.

> iv. After this reign of terror, Laodice set her son (Selecus II) on the throne of the Syrian dominion.

3. (7-9) From the South, an army defeats the kingdom of the North.

But from a branch of her roots *one* shall arise in his place, who shall come with an army, enter the fortress of the king of the North, and deal with them and prevail. And he shall also carry their gods captive to Egypt, with their princes *and* their precious articles of silver and gold; and he shall continue *more* years than the king of the North. Also *the king of the North* shall come to the kingdom of the king of the South, but shall return to his own land.

a. **Who shall come with an army**: The angel told Daniel that a **branch of her roots** would come from the South and **prevail** over the kings of the North.

b. **Deal with them and prevail**: This was fulfilled in the person of Ptolemy III, who was the brother of Berenice (the **branch of her roots**). Avenging the murder of his sister, Ptolemy III invaded Syria and humbled Selecus II.

> i. **He shall continue more years than the king of the North**: Ptolemy III lived four years past Selecus II.

4. (10) The sons of the king of the North and their victory.

However his sons shall stir up strife, and assemble a multitude of great forces; and *one* shall certainly come and overwhelm and pass through; then he shall return to his fortress and stir up strife.

a. **His sons shall stir up strife**: The sons of the kings of the North would continue the battle. One of the sons would conquer the Holy Land (**overwhelm and pass through**) which stood as a buffer between the kings of the South and the kings of the North.

b. **Assemble a multitude of great forces**: This was fulfilled in Seleucus III and Antiochus III, the two sons of Seleucus II. Both were successful generals, but Seleucus III ruled only a short time and was succeeded by his brother.

i. In a furious battle, Antiochus III took back the Holy Land from the dominion of the Ptolemies.

5. (11-12) The king of the South gains an upper hand over the king of the North.

And the king of the South shall be moved with rage, and go out and fight with him, with the king of the North, who shall muster a great multitude; but the multitude shall be given into the hand of his *enemy*. When he has taken away the multitude, his heart will be lifted up; and he will cast down tens of thousands, but he will not prevail.

a. **The king of the South shall be moved with rage**: The angel told Daniel that the king of the South would attack and meet a **great multitude** of soldiers from the king of the North. The king of the North would lose in battle and his **multitude** would be defeated.

b. **He will not prevail**: This was fulfilled when Antiochus III was defeated at the battle of Raphia. Because of that loss he was forced to give back dominion over the Holy Land to Ptolemy IV.

6. (13-16) The king of the North and his occupation of the **Glorious Land**.

For the king of the North will return and muster a multitude greater than the former, and shall certainly come at the end of some years with a great army and much equipment. Now in those times many shall rise up against the king of the South. Also, violent men of your people shall exalt themselves in fulfillment of the vision, but they shall fall. So the king of the North shall come and build a siege mound, and take a fortified city; and the forces of the South shall not withstand *him*. Even his choice troops *shall have* no strength to resist. But he who comes against him shall do according to his own will, and no one shall stand against him. He shall stand in the Glorious Land with destruction in his power.

a. **The king of the North... shall certainly come at the end of some years with a great army**: The angel told Daniel that the northern dynasty would answer back and defeat the king of the South in an extended siege. This victory would give the king of the North dominion over **the Glorious Land**.

    i. "The land of ornaments - that is, Judea, which, lying betwixt these two potent princes, was perpetually afflicted, as corn is ground asunder lying betwixt two heavy millstones." (Trapp)

b. **No one shall stand against him**: This was fulfilled when Antiochus III invaded Egypt again, gaining final control over the armies of Ptolemy V and over the Holy Land.

    i. **Many shall rise up against the king of the South**: Jews living in the Holy Land helped Antiochus III defeat the **king of the South**. This was because the Jewish people resented the rule of the Egyptian Ptolemies (**violent men of your people shall exalt themselves in fulfillment of the vision**).

    ii. **He who comes against him shall do according to his own will... with destruction in his power**: The Jewish people of **the Glorious Land** initially welcomed Antiochus III as a liberator from Egyptian rule. Their decision to support Antiochus III proved unwise when he turned **destruction** upon the **Glorious Land** and its people.

7. (17) The king of the South will give his daughter to the king of the North.

He shall also set his face to enter with the strength of his whole kingdom, and upright ones with him; thus shall he do. And he shall give him the daughter of women to destroy it; but she shall not stand *with him*, or be for him.

a. **He shall also set his face**: The king of the North who ruled over the Holy Land would also attempt to dominate and destroy the king of the South. He would make one attempt by giving the king of the South **the daughter of women to destroy**, but this plot would not succeed.

b. **She shall not stand with him**: This was fulfilled when Antiochus III gave his daughter Cleopatra to Ptolemy V of Egypt. He did this hoping to gain permanent influence and eventually control in Egypt. To the great disappointment of Antiochus III, the plan did not succeed because Cleopatra wasn't faithful to her Egyptian husband at all.

    i. This was not the most famous Cleopatra from ancient history, but this was the ancestor of the more famous Cleopatra. The more famous Egyptian woman lived some 100 years after the time of this Cleopatra.

8. (18-19) The king of the North is stopped and stumbles.

After this he shall turn his face to the coastlands, and shall take many. But a ruler shall bring the reproach against them to an end; and with

the reproach removed, he shall turn back on him. Then he shall turn his
face toward the fortress of his own land; but he shall stumble and fall,
and not be found.

> a. **He shall turn back on him**: After the disappointing effort through the
> daughter Cleopatra, the king of the North would turn his efforts towards
> **the coastlands** - until he was stopped by one formerly under **reproach**,
> until **he shall stumble and fall, and not be found**.

> b. **He shall stumble and fall**: This was fulfilled when Antiochus III turned
> his attention towards the areas of Asia Minor and Greece. He was helped
> by Hannibal, the famous general from Carthage. But a Roman General,
> Lucius Cornelius Scipio, defeated Antiochus in Greece. Antiochus planned
> to humiliate Greece but was humiliated instead. He returned to his former
> regions, having lost all that he gained and died shortly after.

> > i. After this defeat Antiochus III had an inglorious end. Needing
> > money badly for his treasury, he resorted to pillaging a Babylonian
> > temple and was killed by enraged local citizens.

9. (20) The brief reign of the succeeding king of the North.

**There shall arise in his place one who imposes taxes *on* the glorious
kingdom; but within a few days he shall be destroyed, but not in anger
or in battle.**

> a. **There shall arise in his place**: After the inglorious end of the king of the
> North, his successor would raise taxes and meet a soon end.

> b. **One who imposes taxes**: This was fulfilled in the brief reign of Seleucus
> III, the eldest son of Antiochus III. He sought to tax his dominion
> (including the **glorious kingdom**, the Holy Land) to increase revenues.
> His plan to pillage the Jerusalem temple was set aside when his ambassador
> had an angelic vision of warning.

> > i. **Within a few days he shall be destroyed**: Seleucus III was
> > assassinated, probably by his brother Antiochus IV.

C. Antiochus IV, known as Antiochus Epiphanes: *A Vile Person.*

1. (21) The **vile person** comes to power.

**And in his place shall arise a vile person, to whom they will not give the
honor of royalty; but he shall come in peaceably, and seize the kingdom
by intrigue.**

> a. **In his place shall arise a vile person**: The angel told Daniel that after
> the brief reign of the former king of the North, the next king would be **a**
> **vile person**. He would not be recognized as **royalty**, but shall take power
> by **intrigue**.

b. **In his place**: This was fulfilled in the successor of Seleucis III, named Antiochus IV. He did not come to the throne legitimately because it was strongly suspected that he murdered his older brother, the previous king. The other potential heir (the son of Seleucus III) was imprisoned in Rome.

i. **He shall come in peaceably**: Apart from the murder of his older brother, Antiochus IV didn't use terror to gain power. He used flattery, smooth promises and **intrigue**.

ii. "He *flattered Eumenes*, king of Pergamus, and *Attalus* his brother, and got their assistance. He *flattered* the Romans, and sent ambassadors to court their favour, and pay them the arrears of the tribute. He *flattered* the Syrians, and gained their concurrence." (Clarke)

iii. Antiochus IV took the title *Epiphanes*, meaning *illustrious*. Others derisively called him *Epimanes*, meaning *madman*.

2. (22-27) The vile person fails to conquer the king of the South.

With the force of a flood they shall be swept away from before him and be broken, and also the prince of the covenant. And after the league *is made* with him he shall act deceitfully, for he shall come up and become strong with a small *number of* people. He shall enter peaceably, even into the richest places of the province; and he shall do *what* his fathers have not done, nor his forefathers: he shall disperse among them the plunder, spoil, and riches; and he shall devise his plans against the strongholds, but *only* for a time. He shall stir up his power and his courage against the king of the South with a great army. And the king of the South shall be stirred up to battle with a very great and mighty army; but he shall not stand, for they shall devise plans against him. Yes, those who eat of the portion of his delicacies shall destroy him; his army shall be swept away, and many shall fall down slain. Both these kings' hearts *shall be* bent on evil, and they shall speak lies at the same table; but it shall not prosper, for the end *will* still *be* at the appointed time.

a. **He shall act deceitfully**: The angel told Daniel that the new king of the North (the *vile person* of Daniel 11:21) would attempt a deceitful covenant with the king of the South. This would fail, and there would be a great battle that would not change the balance of power.

b. **He shall stir up his power**: This was fulfilled when Antiochus Epiphanes carried on the feud between the dynasties but pretended friendship and alliance to catch them off guard. Despite massive efforts and epic battles, Antiochus Epiphanes did **not stand**, and **his army** was **swept away**.

i. The defeat of Antiochus Epiphanes at his second campaign against Egypt was important, because Egypt beat Antiochus with the help of

Rome. At the end of it all, Antiochus Epiphanes and his kingdom were under the dominion of Rome.

ii. In a famous battle, the Roman Navy defeated the navy of Antiochus Epiphanes. After the battle, a Roman general drew a circle around Antiochus in the dirt and demanded to know if he would surrender and pay tribute to Rome - and demanded to know before he stepped out of the circle. From that point on there was no doubt: Antiochus Epiphanes took his orders from Rome and was under Roman dominion.

iii. **Those who eat of the portion of his delicacies shall destroy him**: This was fulfilled in the treachery against Anitochus IV by his own counselors.

3. (28-35) The vile person turns on the Holy Land with violence.

While returning to his land with great riches, his heart shall be *moved* against the holy covenant; so he shall do *damage* and return to his own land. At the appointed time he shall return and go toward the south; but it shall not be like the former or the latter. For ships from Cyprus shall come against him; therefore he shall be grieved, and return in rage against the holy covenant, and do *damage*. So he shall return and show regard for those who forsake the holy covenant. And forces shall be mustered by him, and they shall defile the sanctuary fortress; then they shall take away the daily *sacrifices*, and place *there* the abomination of desolation. Those who do wickedly against the covenant he shall corrupt with flattery; but the people who know their God shall be strong, and carry out *great exploits*. And those of the people who understand shall instruct many; yet *for many* days they shall fall by sword and flame, by captivity and plundering. Now when they fall, they shall be aided with a little help; but many shall join with them by intrigue. And *some* of those of understanding shall fall, to refine them, purify *them*, and make *them* white, *until* the time of the end; because *it is* still for the appointed time.

a. **His heart shall be moved against the holy covenant**: When the vile person returned to his land, he would attack the land, people, and the temple of Israel. It will be a time of great courage and great treachery among the people of God.

b. **So he shall do damage and return to his own land**: This was fulfilled when Antiochus Epiphanes returned from Egypt, bitter from defeat. He vented his anger against Jerusalem, which was already shaken because Antiochus sold the office of High Priest and persecuted the Jewish people to conform to Greek culture, forsaking the faith and traditions of their fathers.

i. **While returning to his land with great riches**: Failing in his invasion of Egypt, Antiochus Epiphanes returned home with only great plunder to soothe his wounded pride.

ii. **Ships from Cyprus shall come against him**: This was naval assistance from the Romans, who helped the Egyptians turn back Antiochus Epiphanes.

iii. **They shall take away the daily sacrifices, and place there the abomination of desolation**: Antiochus Epiphanes set up an image of Zeus at the temple altar. He demanded sacrifice to this image, and later desecrated the temple by sacrificing a pig on it. "It was in truth an abomination, which brought a desolate condition to the Temple, for now no one would come to worship at all." (Wood)

iv. **Those who do wickedly against the covenant he shall corrupt with flattery; but the people who know their God shall be strong**: When Antiochus Epiphanes turned on Jerusalem, the Jewish people were divided. Some forsook their covenant with God and embraced Greek culture. Those who knew their God made a stand for righteousness in the face of incredible persecution.

v. **For many days they shall fall by sword and flame, by captivity and plundering**: In his attack on Jerusalem Antiochus IV is said to have killed 80,000 Jews, taken 40,000 more as prisoners, and sold another 40,000 as slaves. He also plundered the temple, robbing it of approximately $1 billion by modern calculations.

vi. **Until the time of the end; because it is still for the appointed time**: This terror could only last for as long as God had appointed it, and God had a purpose even for such persecution and blasphemy.

D. The Antichrist: the end times Antiochus Epiphanes.

1. (36) The willful king: a shift to a future fulfillment.

Then the king shall do according to his own will: he shall exalt and magnify himself above every god, shall speak blasphemies against the God of gods, and shall prosper till the wrath has been accomplished; for what has been determined shall be done.

a. **He shall exalt and magnify himself above every god**: The angel explained to Daniel that this king would blaspheme God and exalt himself until **the wrath has been accomplished** and **what has been determined shall be done.**

b. **Above every god**: Here we shift from what *was* fulfilled in the Ptolemies and the Selucids to what *will* be fulfilled in the Antichrist, the final world dictator. Daniel was told that this revelation pertained to *the latter days* (Daniel 10:14), and Daniel 11:36 begins to look more towards this final world dictator, who is sort of a "last days Antiochus Epiphanes."

i. We know that everything about this prophecy was not fulfilled during the career of Antiochus Epiphanes. Jesus specifically said the *real* abomination of desolation was still in the future (Matthew 24:15). The Apostle Paul paraphrased Daniel 11:36 in reference to the coming Antichrist: *Let no one deceive you by any means; for that Day will not come unless the falling away comes first, and the man of sin is revealed, the son of perdition, who opposes and exalts himself above all that is called God or that is worshiped, so that he sits as God in the temple of God, showing himself that he is God* (2 Thessalonians 2:3-4).

ii. Antiochus Epiphanes is important, but mostly as a historical preview of the Antichrist. This is why so much space is given to describing the career of one evil man - because he prefigures the ultimate evil man. Antiochus Epiphanes is the "trailer" released well before the Antichrist, who is like the "feature."

c. **He shall exalt and magnify himself above every god**: Antiochus Epiphanes certainly did this in the general sense that all sinners oppose God. Yet he remained loyal to the Greek religious tradition, which revered the entire Olympian pantheon. Antiochus Epiphanes put a statue of Zeus in the temple, not of *himself*. This statement will be far more precisely fulfilled in the Antichrist, who *sits as God in the temple of God, showing himself that he is God* (2 Thessalonians 2:4).

d. **Shall prosper till the wrath has been accomplished**: Antichrist will do much damage, but he is on a short chain and will only work into God's plan. God's purpose will be **accomplished**.

2. (37-39) The character and authority of the "willful king."

He shall regard neither the God of his fathers nor the desire of women, nor regard any god; for he shall exalt himself above *them* all. But in their place he shall honor a god of fortresses; and a god which his fathers did not know he shall honor with gold and silver, with precious stones and pleasant things. Thus he shall act against the strongest fortresses with a foreign god, which he shall acknowledge, *and* advance *its* glory; and he shall cause them to rule over many, and divide the land for gain.

a. **He shall regard neither the God of his fathers nor the desire of women**: Based on this, some Bible scholars believe that the Antichrist will be of Jewish descent, and perhaps will also be a homosexual. These things may not be popularly known about the man, but they may be true nonetheless.

i. But many commentators believe that **the desire of women** refers to Jesus, in that all women desired the honor of bearing the Messiah and understanding "desire" as it is used in Haggai 2:7. Seeing **the desire of women** as Jesus makes most sense in light of the flow of context.

b. **He shall honor a god of fortresses**: The Antichrist will take and hold power with military might and the shrewd use of great riches.

3. (40-45) The final conflict.

At the time of the end the king of the South shall attack him; and the king of the North shall come against him like a whirlwind, with chariots, horsemen, and with many ships; and he shall enter the countries, overwhelm *them*, and pass through. He shall also enter the Glorious Land, and many *countries* shall be overthrown; but these shall escape from his hand: Edom, Moab, and the prominent people of Ammon. He shall stretch out his hand against the countries, and the land of Egypt shall not escape. He shall have power over the treasures of gold and silver, and over all the precious things of Egypt; also the Libyans and Ethiopians *shall follow* at his heels. But news from the east and the north shall trouble him; therefore he shall go out with great fury to destroy and annihilate many. And he shall plant the tents of his palace between the seas and the glorious holy mountain; yet he shall come to his end, and no one will help him.

a. **At the time of the end**: The angel described to Daniel a confederation of kings coming against this great leader, with a battle in and near the Holy Land.

b. **King of the South shall attack him; and the king of the North shall come against him like a whirlwind**: Prophetically speaking, a precise identification of peoples mentioned is difficult. The **king of the South** may be Egypt or represent the Arab community. The **king of the North** may be the Antichrist's domain (as the "new Antiochus Epiphanes") or it may be Russia.

i. The precise points may be cloudy, but the general idea is clear. The end will be marked by great conflict, culminating in the world's armies gathering in the Promised Land to do final battle.

c. **Yet he shall come to his end, and no one will help him**: In the end there is no hope for the Antichrist or for any of his followers.

Daniel 12 - Israel's Time of Trouble

A. The time of trouble destined for Israel.

1. (1a) A future **time of trouble** for Israel.

"At that time Michael shall stand up,
The great prince who stands *watch* **over the sons of your people;**
And there shall be a time of trouble,
Such as never was since there was a nation,
***Even* to that time.**

> a. **At that time**: This does not mean that what is described in Daniel 12:1 happened immediately after what the events in Daniel 11:36-45. It means that it happened in the same era.

> b. **Michael shall stand up**: The angel **Michael** is often associated with spiritual battle (Daniel 10:13, Daniel 10:21, Jude 1:9, and Revelation 12:7). Since Michael is called *the archangel* (Jude 1:9), he is Satan's true opposite. Satan is not the opposite of Jesus; he is the opposite of Michael, this high-ranking angel.

> c. **The great prince who stands watch over the sons of your people**: In addition to his role as a spiritual warrior, Michael has a special job in protecting Israel. God appointed Michael as a spiritual guardian over Israel.

> d. **There shall be a time of trouble**: This refers to the time of persecution for Israel and world calamity known as the Great Tribulation. This period is also called *the time of Jacob's trouble* in Jeremiah 30:7.

> e. **Such as never was since there was a nation, even to that time**: The Jewish people have known many a **time of trouble** through their history. From the horrors at the fall of Samaria and Jerusalem to the terrors wrought by Antiochus Epiphanes, to the destruction of Jerusalem by the Romans, to the persecutions from the church during the Dark Ages, to the pogroms of Europe, to the 20th Century Holocaust, it often seems that all

Israel's history has been a **time of trouble**. Yet this **time of trouble** will be different. This will be a *worse* **time of trouble** than Israel has ever seen before.

i. Jesus quoted this passage in Matthew 24:21: *For then there will be great tribulation, such as has not been since the beginning of the world until this time, no, nor ever shall be.* With great sadness, we must say that the Bible teaches that the worst has yet to come for Israel and the Jewish people.

ii. This phrase "establishes its connection with the final or 'great' tribulation above mentioned, for there can manifestly be only *one* 'time of trouble, such as never was since there was a nation even to that same time.' " (Newell)

iii. Revelation 12:13-17 tells us what makes this time so terrible. It describes the fury of the devil directed against the Jewish people during this time. The trumpets, seals, and bowls of Revelation all described the horrific conditions of the world in general during this time. The Jewish people will be targets of the full fury of the devil and his antichrist during this period, and will live in a world that is in incredible upheaval because of the judgment of God.

iv. "The Jew has always been a target of Satan. He has sought to destroy them because he knew that God has ordained to accomplish His purposes through this nation. And thus Satan has attempted in times past to destroy the nation of Israel in order to thwart the purposes of God." (Smith)

2. (1b) A promise of deliverance.

And at that time your people shall be delivered,
Every one who is found written in the book.

a. **And at that time your people shall be delivered**: Despite the terrors of that time, deliverance is assured. No matter how great the attack is against the Jewish people, God promises to preserve them. He will never break His promise to Abraham: *And I will establish My covenant between Me and you and your descendants after you in their generations, for an everlasting covenant, to be God to you and your descendants after you* (Genesis 17:7).

b. **Every one who is found written in the book**: This promise of deliverance is not for every last person of Jewish heritage, but for these who are **found written in the book**. Not every person of Jewish heritage will be saved, yet Israel as a whole will be known as a people who trust in Jesus as their Messiah, and truly turn to the Lord (Romans 11:25-27).

B. The resolution of resurrection.

1. (2) The resurrection of the dead.

And many of those who sleep in the dust of the earth shall awake,
Some to everlasting life,
Some to shame *and* everlasting contempt.

a. **Many of those who sleep in the dust of the earth shall awake**: Some think this refers to the resurrection of Israel as a *nation*. But the plainest meaning is that it refers to the resurrection of the body in general.

b. **Some to everlasting life, some to shame and everlasting contempt**: The Bible clearly teaches two resurrections, one for the saved and one for the damned (John 5:29, Revelation 20:4-6, and Revelation 11-15). If we really believed *every one of us would live forever*, it would profoundly change our life.

i. **Everlasting contempt**: The terror of hell never ends. There is not blissful annihilation after some period of punishment. This passage denies a rising doctrine within the church: a modified annihilationism that teaches that unjustified sinners are sent to Hell and they suffer torment for a while, but then their beings perish for eternity.

ii. Revelation 20:10 also certainly describes *eternal* punishment for the Devil and the Antichrist. "There would be no way possible in the Greek language to state more emphatically the everlasting punishment of the lost than here in mentioning both day and night and the expression 'forever and ever,' literally 'to the ages of ages.' " (Walvoord)

iii. Logically, Hell *must* be eternal, because it is where imperfect beings must pay a continual penalty for their sins because they cannot ever make a perfect payment. Principles behind Old Testament sacrifice remind us that an *imperfect* payment for sins must be a *continual* payment for sins.

c. **Many of those who sleep in the dust of the earth shall awake**: The Scriptures as a whole teach us that there are not *only* **many** resurrected. There is evidence that the Hebrew word for **many** in Daniel 12:2 can also be used for *all*. "The emphasis is not upon many as opposed to all, but rather on the numbers involved." (Baldwin)

i. As well, the Bible states that all are raised but not all at the same time or in the same manner (Revelation 20:5-6).

ii. "The wicked also shall 'come forth,' but by another principle, and for another purpose; they shall come out of their graves like filthy toads against this terrible storm." (Trapp)

2. (3) A promise for the righteous.

**Those who are wise shall shine
Like the brightness of the firmament,
And those who turn many to righteousness
Like the stars forever and ever.**

a. **Those who are wise shall shine like the brightness of the firmament**: Those who live in God's wisdom will **shine**. Despite the entire calamity, all the difficulty coming upon Israel, God has **those who are wise**, and they **shall shine**.

b. **And those who turn many to righteousness like the stars**: Here, the wise among God's people are those who **turn many to righteousness**.

i. All God's people are like **stars** in the sense that they radiate light and help others to see and find their way. But certainly, those **who turn many to righteousness** shine even more brightly, helping even more people to see the light and find their way.

ii. This promise applies to all the wise, and all of those who **turn many to righteousness** through all ages. But it may have its most specific application to the 144,000 evangelists from Israel's tribes during the Tribulation (Revelation 7).

c. **Forever and ever**: The brightness of God's wise ones, and those who **turn many to righteousness**, will last forever. It isn't fading. It endures, when so many other things that we put our effort into, even if they succeed, give only a temporary "shine." It is worth it to invest our lives into the things that last **forever and ever.**

C. Conclusion of the book.

1. (4) Instructions to seal the book.

"But you, Daniel, shut up the words, and seal the book until the time of the end; many shall run to and fro, and knowledge shall increase."

a. **Shut up the words, and seal the book**: To **shut up the words** implied that the words should be kept safely until the time when they were needed. **Seal the book** has the double sense of authenticating the message and preserving it.

b. **Until the time of the end**: Daniel's prophecy certainly was of some value in his own day. But there would come a day, **the time of the end**, when his prophecy would be of even more importance. Therefore, it was important to **shut up the words, and seal the book until the time of the end.**

i. "We must wait 'till the time of the end;' and this, it appears from the following calculations, will not arrive before the TWENTIETH CENTURY. We here see the reason why these prophecies are at present so imperfectly understood. *God has sealed them.*" (Adam Clarke, 1825)

c. **Many shall run to and fro, and knowledge shall increase**: Here, Daniel describes a characteristic of **the time of the end**. Many take this prediction as being fulfilled in the travel (**run to and fro**) and information explosions (**knowledge shall increase**) of our modern age.

> i. **Many shall run to and fro, and knowledge shall increase**: This has more the idea of *searching after knowledge* rather than *rapid forms of transportation*.

> ii. "The idea is that people would run about trying to find answers to important questions, especially in reference to future events." (Wood)

> iii. "The correct sense is that 'many shall search it through and through,' and that as a consequence 'knowledge of the book itself shall be increased.' " (Newell)

d. **Shut up the words, and seal the book**: Daniel has revealed enough to us so that the book really can be sealed. From Daniel 11:36 to Daniel 12:3, we see:

- A world ruler, utterly opposed to God.
- A world religion, based on the abomination of desolation.
- A world war, which defeats the ruler.
- A time of great tribulation for Israel lasting three and one-half years.
- Deliverance for the people of God after the tribulation.
- Resurrection and judgment.
- The reward of the righteous.

2. (5-7) How long will the time of trouble be?

Then I, Daniel, looked; and there stood two others, one on this riverbank and the other on that riverbank. And *one* said to the man clothed in linen, who *was* above the waters of the river, "How long shall the fulfillment of these wonders *be*?" Then I heard the man clothed in linen, who *was* above the waters of the river, when he held up his right hand and his left hand to heaven, and swore by Him who lives forever, that *it shall be* for a time, times, and half *a time;* and when the power of the holy people has been completely shattered, all these *things* shall be finished.

a. **Two others, one on this riverbank and the other on that riverbank**: Daniel is back to the **riverbank** first mentioned in Daniel 10:4. The visions of Daniel 10 through 12 all took place as Daniel stood at this **riverbank**.

b. **One said to the man clothed in linen... "How long shall the fulfillment of these wonders be?"** Seemingly, these other men on the riverbank were angels. One angel asked the other, not for the benefit of the angel, but for Daniel's benefit and our benefit.

c. **Held up his right hand and his left hand to heaven, and swore by Him who lives forever**: In a solemn oath, one angel announced that the time of trouble would last three and one-half years (**a time, times, and half a time**).

> i. The prediction was *emphasized* by the solemn oath, and by the miracle that accompanied the words: **who was above the waters in the river**. The angel "walked on water" when he told the other angel and Daniel that these things would happen within a three and one half year period.

d. **A time, times, and half a time**: This three and one-half year period is well known in other passages of Biblical prophecy.

- Daniel 7:25 described it as the period that saints are given into Antichrist's hands.

- Daniel 9:27 described it as the period between the breaking of Antichrist's covenant with Israel, the erection of the abomination of desolation, and the establishment of Jesus' kingdom.

- Daniel 12:7 described it as the duration of "the time of trouble" for Israel.

- Revelation 11:2 described it as the period that the holy city will be tread underfoot by Gentiles.

- Revelation 11:3 described it as the period of ministry for the two witnesses.

- Revelation 12:6 and 12:14 described it as the period that Israel (perhaps only its remnant) is preserved by God in the wilderness.

- Revelation 13:5 describe it as the duration of Antichrist's authority to rule, persecute and blaspheme.

> i. Taking all these together, we are obviously dealing with the last half of Daniel's seventieth week (the Great Tribulation); and we know very little about the first half.

e. **When the power of the holy people has been completely shattered, all these things shall be finished**: The people of Israel will seem completely crushed as these things end, but at that time, the Messiah – upon whom they will trust before He returns – will return to rescue them.

3. (8) Daniel's last question: how will it all turn out?

Although I heard, I did not understand. Then I said, "My lord, what *shall be* the end of these *things?"*

a. **Although I heard, I did not understand**: This comforts us. Daniel didn't understand it all either, even though he heard it first hand.

b. **What shall be the end of these things?** Perhaps Daniel asked this question because he was anxious, as he understood just how terrible the time of trouble would be.

4. (9-13) Answer: God will purify and preserve His people, and has set a limit of days to the time of trouble.

And he said, "Go *your way*, Daniel, for the words *are* closed up and sealed till the time of the end. Many shall be purified, made white, and refined, but the wicked shall do wickedly; and none of the wicked shall understand, but the wise shall understand. And from the time *that* the daily *sacrifice* is taken away, and the abomination of desolation is set up, *there shall be* one thousand two hundred and ninety days. Blessed *is* he who waits, and comes to the one thousand three hundred and thirty-five days. But you, go *your way* till the end; for you shall rest, and will arise to your inheritance at the end of the days."

a. **Go your way, Daniel**: The command to **go your way** is literally merely "to go" but it is not meant physically. The angel told Daniel to make a mental departure from the questioning. More details would be revealed later; but Daniel must be content with what God has revealed thus far.

b. **For the words are closed up and sealed till the time of the end**: Daniel must make a *mental* departure from his questioning, because the revealing of these things will not come **till the time of the end**. Until then, there is a sense in which these prophecies **are closed up and sealed**.

i. We shouldn't think there was no instruction, no blessing, or no benefit in these words for any generation until the **time of the end**. But the meaning of these prophecies would be *less* mysterious at **the time of the end**.

ii. The massive interest in prophecy, and the incredible development in understanding of Biblical prophecy in the last 150 years should make us see that we truly are at **the time of the end**.

iii. One of the common arguments against some understandings of Biblical prophecy is "Your ideas are new. The early church or Christians through the ages didn't teach these things. Your ideas are wrong because they are new." But this word to Daniel, that **the words are closed up and sealed till the time of the end** should make us think differently.

iv. Additionally, when we look at Church history, we see that God has successively had the church focus on specific areas of doctrine at different periods. Our present understanding of many areas of Biblical teaching were only most carefully and precisely defined *after* God appointed the church to focus on that doctrinal area.

v. For example, in the second through fourth centuries, the church focused on the doctrine of Scripture. In the fourth century, the focus was on the doctrine of God (in the Trinity). In the fifth century, the focus was on the doctrine of Christ. In the fifth through seventh centuries, the focus was on the doctrine of man. In the fifteenth and seventeenth centuries, the focus was on the doctrine of salvation. In the sixteenth and seventeenth centuries, the focus was on the doctrine of the church. So it should not surprise us that it was not until the nineteenth and twentieth centuries - **the time of the end** - that the focus would turn upon the doctrine of last things and the return of Jesus.

c. **Many shall be purified, made white, and refined**: This is another prediction for what was future to Daniel, because this degree of purification is only possible *after* the finished work of Jesus on the cross.

d. **But the wicked shall do wickedly**: Most specifically, we would say that this prediction has to do with the end times, when wickedness will abound more than ever (as in the Antichrist and his government), but an innumerable multitude will also be saved (as is seen in Revelation 7:9-10).

e. **And from the time that the daily sacrifice is taken away, and the abomination of desolation is set up, there shall be one thousand two hundred and ninety days**: This was an amazingly specific prophecy. Daniel said that from the time of the **abomination of desolation**, you can simply start marking off your calendar to the final consummation of all things, 1,290 days later.

i. This is why Jesus pointed to Daniel's prophecy of the **abomination of desolation** as *the sign* that would mark the immediacy of His return (Matthew 24:15).

f. **Blessed is he who waits, and comes to the one thousand three hundred and thirty-five days**: It is difficult to say what the relationship is between the three and one-half years mentioned in many places and the 1,335 days mentioned here. We could say that at the end of the 1,260 days Jesus returns. At the end of the 1,290 days, Jesus' government is officially installed. At the end of the 1,335 days the nations are judged (Matthew 25:31-46).

> i. "It is quite possible that this period of judgment of those that have lived through the tribulation period and have survived somehow during this holocaust when God's judgment will be poured out upon the earth, when they are brought to stand before Jesus at this judgment, that this judgment of the Lord will take a forty-five day period." (Smith)

g. **But you, go your way till the end**: Daniel's mind was filled with exciting and frightening prophetic thoughts. Perhaps it was easy for those things to become a distraction instead of a blessing to him. So the angel concluded with an important reminder: **go your way till the end**. God had a course He wanted Daniel to complete, and Daniel needed to remain focused on *that*.

> i. Adam Clarke draws the following points from Daniel 12:13:
>
> - Every man has his **way** to go.
> - Every man has an **end**.
> - There is a **rest** provided for the people of God.
> - There is an **inheritance** for the people of God.

> ii. At the end of the gospel of John, Jesus told Peter about his destiny to die as a martyr for Jesus. Peter wanted to know about John's destiny, so he asked Jesus, "What about John?" Essentially, Jesus replied, "It's none of your business. You follow Me" (John 21:22). In the same way, Daniel was not to spend all of his time and energy speculating and worrying about things he couldn't know. Instead, he should simply obey the word to go your way till the end - something we must all do.

Appendix A - *The Terrors of Antiochus IV as Described in 1 Maccabees*

And after two years fully expired the king sent his chief collector of tribute unto the cities of Juda, who came unto Jerusalem with a great multitude, and spake peaceable words unto them, but all was deceit: for when they had given him credence, he fell suddenly upon the city, and smote it very sore, and destroyed much people of Israel. And when he had taken the spoils of the city, he set it on fire, and pulled down the houses and walls thereof on every side. But the women and children took they captive, and possessed the cattle. (1 Maccabees 1:29-32)

Then many of the people were gathered unto them, to wit every one that forsook the law; and so they committed evils in the land; and drove the Israelites into secret places, even wheresoever they could flee for succour. Now the fifteenth day of the month Casleu, in the hundred forty and fifth year, they set up the abomination of desolation upon the altar, and builded idol altars throughout the cities of Juda on every side; and burnt incense at the doors of their houses, and in the streets. And when they had torn in pieces the books of the law which they found, they burnt them with fire. And whosoever was found with any book of the testament, or if any committed to the law, the king's commandment was, that they should put him to death. Thus did they by their authority unto the Israelites every month, to as many as were found in the cities. Now the five and twentieth day of the month they did sacrifice upon the idol altar, which was upon the altar of God. At which time according to the commandment they put to death certain women, that had caused their children to be circumcised. And they hanged the infants about their necks, and rifled their houses, and slew them that had circumcised them. (1 Maccabees 1:52-61)

Moreover king Antiochus wrote to his whole kingdom, that all should be one people, and every one should leave his laws: so all the heathen agreed according to the commandment of the king. Yea, many also of the Israelites consented to his religion, and sacrificed unto idols, and profaned the sabbath. For the king had sent letters by messengers unto Jerusalem and the cities of Juda that they should follow the strange laws of the land, and forbid burnt offerings, and sacrifice, and drink offerings, in the temple; and that they should profane the sabbaths and festival days, and pollute the sanctuary and holy people: set up altars, and groves, and chapels of idols, and sacrifice swine's flesh, and unclean beasts: That they should also leave their children uncircumcised, and make their souls abominable with all manner of uncleanness and profanation, to the end they might forget the law, and change all the ordinances. And whosoever would not do according to the commandment of the king, he said, he should die. (1 Maccabees 1:41-50)

Appendix B - Alexander the Great and Daniel's Prophecy, Described by Josephus

Now Alexander, when he had taken Gaza, made haste to go up to Jerusalem; and Jaddua the high priest, when he heard that, was in an agony, and under terror, as not knowing how he should meet the Macedonians, since the king was displeased at his forgoing disobedience. He therefore ordained that the people should make supplications, and should join with him in offering sacrifices to God, whom he besought to protect that nation, and to deliver them from the perils that were coming upon them; whereupon God warned him in a dream, which came upon him after he had offered sacrifice, that he should take courage, and adorn the city, and open the gates; that the rest appear in white garments, but that he and the priests should meet the king in the habits proper to their order, without the dread of any ill consequences, which the providence of God would prevent. Upon which, when he rose from his sleep, he greatly rejoiced; and declared to all the warning he had received from God. According to which dream he acted entirely, and so waited for the coming of the king.

And when he understood that he was not far from the city, he went out in procession, with the priests and the multitude of the citizens. The procession was venerable, and the manner of it different from that of other nations.... [The approaching army] thought they should have liberty to plunder the city, and torment the high priest to death, which the king's displeasure fairly promised them, the very reverse of it happened; for Alexander, when he saw the multitude at a distance, in white garments, while the priests stood clothed with fine linen, and the high-priest in purple and scarlet clothing, with his mitre on his head having the golden plate on which the name of God was engraved, he approached by himself, and adored that name, and first saluted the high-priest.

The Jews also did all together, with one voice, salute Alexander, and encompass him about : whereupon the kings of Syria and the rest were surprised at what Alexander had done, and supposed him disordered in his mind. However, Parmenio alone went up to him, and asked him how it came to pass, that when all others adored him, he should adore the high-priest of the Jews? To whom he replied, "I did not adore him, but that God who hath honored him with that high-priesthood, for I saw this very person in a dream, in this very habit, when I was at Dios, in Macedonia, who, when I was considering with myself how I might obtain the dominion of Asia, exhorted me to make no delay, but boldly to pass over the sea thither, for that he would conduct my army, and would give me the dominion over the Persians; whence it is, that having seen no other in that habit, and now seeing this person in it, and remembering that vision and the exhortation which I had in my dream, I believe that I bring this army under the divine conduct, and shall therewith conquer Darius, and destroy the power of the Persians, and that all things will succeed according to what is in my own mind."

And when he had said this to Parmenio, and had given the high-priest his right hand, the priests ran along by him, and he came into the city; and when he went up into the temple, he offered sacrifice to God, according to the high-priest's direction, and magnificently treated both the high priest and the priests. And when the book of Daniel was showed him, wherein Daniel declared that one of the Greeks should destroy the empire of the Persians, he supposed that himself was the person intended; and as he was then glad, he dismissed the multitude for the present, but the next day he called them to him, and bade them ask what favors they pleased of him: whereupon the high-priest desired that they might enjoy the laws of their forefathers, and might pay no tribute on the seventh year. He granted all they desired: and when they entreated him that he would permit the Jews in Babylon and Media to enjoy their own laws also, he willingly promised to do hereafter what they desired.

Josephus, *Antiquities of the Jews*, book XI, chapter 8

The Book of Daniel - Bibliography

Anderson, Sir Robert *The Coming Prince* (Grand Rapids, Michigan: Kregel Publications, 1957)

Archer, Gleason L. "Daniel," *The Expositor's Bible Commentary, Volume 7* (Grand Rapids, Michigan: Zondervan, 1985)

Baldwin, Joyce G. *Daniel, An Introduction and Commentary* (Downer's Grove, Illinois: Inter-Varsity Press, 1978)

Barnes, Albert *Notes on the Old Testament, Daniel Volumes I and II* (Grand Rapids, Michigan: Baker, 1975)

Calvin, John *Commentaries on the Book of the Prophet Daniel Volumes I and II* (Grand Rapids, Michigan: Baker, 1979)

Clarke, Adam *The Holy Bible, Containing the Old and New Testaments, with A Commentary and Critical Notes, Volume IV – Isaiah to Malachi* (New York: Eaton and Mains, 1827?)

Ginzberg, Louis *The Legends of the Jews, Volumes 1-7* (Philadelphia: The Jewish Publication Society of America, 1968)

Heslop, W.G. *Diamonds From Daniel* (Grand Rapids, Michigan: Kregel Publications, 1979)

Ironside, H.A. *Daniel* (Neptune, New Jersey: Loizeaux Brothers, 1988)

Keil, C.F. "Biblical Commentary on the Book of Daniel," *Keil-Delitzsch Commentary on the Old Testament, Volume 9* (Grand Rapids, Michigan: Eerdmans, 1983)

Lowe, Rev. Marmion L. *Christ In the Book of Daniel* (Broome County, New York: Lowe, 1968)

Maclaren, Alexander *Expostions of Holy Scripture, Volume Six* (Grand Rapids, Michigan: Baker, 1984)

Meyer, F.B. *Our Daily Homily* (Westwood, New Jersey: Revell, 1966)

Morgan, G. Campbell *Searchlights from the Word* (New York: Revell, 1926)

Morgan, G. Campbell *An Exposition of the Whole Bible* (Old Tappan, New Jersey: Revell, 1959)

Newell, Philip R. *Daniel: The Man Greatly Beloved and His Prophecies* (Chicago, Moody Press, 1951)

Poole, Matthew *A Commentary on the Holy Bible, Volume 2* (London, Banner of Truth Trust, 1968)

Spence, H.D.M. *The Pulpit Commentary Volume 13: Daniel, Hosea and Joel* (McLean, Virginia: MacDonald, ?)

Spurgeon, Charles Haddon *The New Park Street Pulpit, Volumes 1-6* and *The Metropolitan Tabernacle Pulpit, Volumes 7-63* (Pasadena, Texas: Pilgrim Publications, 1990)

Strauss, Lehman *Daniel* (Neptune, New Jersey: Loizeaux Brothers, 1985)

Talbot, Louis T. *The Prophecies of Daniel* (Wheaton, Illinois: Van Kampen Press, 1954)

Trapp, John *A Commentary on the Old and New Testaments, Volume 3 – Proverbs to Daniel* (Eureka, California: Tanski Publications, 1997)

Walvoord, John F. *Daniel: The Key to Prophetic Revelation* (Chicago, Illinois: Moody Press, 1971)

Wood, Leon *A Commentary on Daniel* (Grand Rapids, Michigan: Zondervan, 1973)

Ricky Ryan is a friend to many; I am happy to be one of them. His friendship and example over the years has been a blessing and I hope an influence upon me. Two great qualities in Daniel - integrity and vision - also mark Ricky. Thank you, Ricky.

Once again I have happily depended on the proofreading help of Martina Patrick. It's just one more way that Martina and Tim show their kindness and friendship to us over many years. Thanks especially for all your prayers and support.

I am often amazed at the remarkable kindness of others, and thanks to all who give the gift of encouragement. With each year that passes, faithful friends and supporters become all the more precious. Through you all, God has been better to me than I have ever deserved.

David Guzik

David Guzik's Bible commentary is regularly used and trusted by many thousands who want to know the Bible better. Pastors, teachers, class leaders, and everyday Christians find his commentary helpful for their own understanding and explanation of the Bible. David and his wife Inga-Lill live in Santa Barbara, California.

You can email David at
david@enduringword.com

For more resources by David Guzik,
go to www.enduringword.com

CPSIA information can be obtained
at www.ICGtesting.com
Printed in the USA
LVHW031751260121
677549LV00005B/981

9 781565 99036